THE BETTER RELATIONSHIP GUIDE FOR WORK, LIFE, FRIENDSHIPS AND INTIMACY

LEARN EFFECTIVE COMMUNICATION SKILLS, SET HEALTHY BOUNDARIES AND DEVELOP IRRESISTIBLE CHARISMA. WITTY BANTER TIPS INCLUDED

CASSANDRA MCBRIDE

© Copyright 2023 – Cassandra McBride. All rights reserved.

It is not legal to reproduce, duplicate, or transmit any part of this document in either electronic means or in printed format. Recording of this publication is strictly prohibited and any storage of this document is not allowed unless with written permission from the publisher except for the use of brief quotations in a book review.

Disclaimer Notice:

Please note the information contained within this book is for educational and entertainment purposes only. All effort has been executed to present accurate, up-to-date, reliable, and complete information but no warranties of any kind are declared or implied. Readers acknowledge that the author is not engaged in the rendering of legal, financial, medical, or professional advice. The content within this book has been derived from various sources that were verifiable at the time.

By reading this notice, the reader agrees that under no circumstances is the author responsible for any losses, direct or indirect, that are incurred because of the use of the information contained within this book, including, but not limited to, errors, omissions, or inaccuracies

Special Bonus!

Want access to the below books for *free*?

Get **Free** Unlimited Access to both of my prior two books by subscribing to my fan base below!

CONTENTS

Introduction 9

Part I
CREATE CLARITY

1 RELATIONSHIPS ARE INEVITABLE 14

The Concept of Clarity 15
What Are Human Relationships? 16
Characteristics of Relationships 17
No One Can Live Alone 18
The Beauty of Companionship 21
Types of Relationships and Their Effects on Your Life 22
What Does True Friendship Look Like? 24

2 PEOPLE ARE COMPLICATED 27

Why Are People So Complicated? 28
The Role That Temperament Plays in a Person 30
We All Have Different Temperaments 32
Meet the Melancholy Human 32
Sanguine 32
Phlegmatics 33
Cholerics 34
How to Adapt to Different Humans with Different Temperaments 35
Determine a Person's Temperament Just by Asking Them a Few Questions 36

3 DEFINING WHAT YOU WANT 41

Taking Interest in Other People 42
Approach Relationships with Clear Intentions 42
What Are Your Goals for Different Relationships? 44
Why You Must Define Your Relationships with Others 47
Defining What Your Relationships with Coworkers Will Look Like 48

Defining Your Relationship with Your Family and Relatives 49
Setting Goals for Your Romantic Relationships 51
Deciding Which Relationships/Friendships Are Truly Worth Keeping 53

4 KNOW AND LOVE YOURSELF FIRST 57

    How Well Do You Know Yourself? 58
    Responding to Life More Effectively 58
    Getting to Love and Accept Yourself 61
    Your Relationships Should Benefit You, Not Harm You 64
    The Five People in Your Life 66
    Love Yourself First to Love Others 67

Part II

COMMUNICATE EFFECTIVELY

5 COMMUNICATION IS EVERYTHING 70

Honing the Art of Communication: The 80/20 Rule 71
Modulating Communication: The Key to Connection 71
Learning from the Masters: The Chameleon Skills of Communication 72
Why Do People Have Communication Issues? 73
Empathy 74
Understanding Empathy: The Practical Perspective 75
Enhancing Non-Verbal Communication: Four Practical Techniques 77
Recognizing Communication Issues in Your Relationships 78
How to Fix Common Communication Issues 80

6 THE POWER OF LISTENING 84

Types of Listening 85
Active Listening 85
How to Practice Active Listening 87
Expanding our Emotional Vocabulary: The Power of Feeling Words 89
Couples and Listening: Bridging the Gap with Empathetic Deep Listening 90

7 OVERCOMING COMMUNICATION CHALLENGES 94

Common Communication Challenges in Relationships 96
Common Communication Challenges at Work 100
Common Communication Challenges with Friends 102

PART III
OVERCOME OBSTACLES

8 SETTING BOUNDARIES 106
- How to Set Boundaries with Family Members 109
- Setting Healthy Boundaries with Colleagues and Bosses 109
- Setting Boundaries with Friends 110
- Setting Boundaries in Your Romantic Relationships 113
- Why Is It Difficult to Accept Boundary Settings? 114

9 HOW TO STOP OVERTHINKING 116
- The Roots of Overthinking 117
- Negative Self-Talk: The Fuel for Overthinking 118
- Understanding the Consequences of Overthinking 119
- Overthinking in Relationships 120
- Dealing with Overthinking - Easy Ways and Methods 121
- Practical Exercise 122

10 DEALING WITH DIFFICULT PEOPLE 124
- Dealing with Difficult Coworkers 126
- Dealing with Difficult Friends 128
- Dealing with Difficult Family Members 130
- Dealing with Difficult Partners 131
- Overcoming the Effects of Dealing with Difficult People 132

PART IV
BE REMARKABLE

11 DEVELOPING FRIENDSHIPS 136
- The Friendship Recession 136
- Why Is Having High Quality Friends So Important? 138
- The Difference Between True Friends and Fake Friends 139
- Where to Meet New People and Make Friends 141
- How to Grow and Build a Healthy Friendship 142
- When Is It Time to Cut Off an Old Friendship for Good? 147

12 UNLEASHING YOUR CHARISMA 148
How To Unleash Your Charisma 151
Verbal Tactics 151
Non-Verbal Tactics 154
Bonus Tactics: Additional Techniques to Enrich Your Conversations 155

13 RULES OF INTIMACY TO LIVE BY 157
Rule number 1: Keep Your Circle Small 157
Rule number 2: Give 100 Percent Commitment to Those You Love 158
Rule number 3: Cut Off Toxic Relationships 158
Rule number 4: Spend Alone Time Together without Social Media 159
Rule number 5: Forgive When You're Offended 160
Rule number *6*: Improve Yourself Daily - Keep Being Valuable and Wanted ... 161
Rule number 7: Embrace Vulnerability in Your Relationships 162

14 WITTY BANTER TIPS AND TECHNIQUES 165
How to Use Witty Banter in Conversation 167
Time-Tested Techniques to Enhance Your Conversational Banter 170
The Power of Open-Ended Questions 170
The Charm of the Double Entendre 170
The Playful Misunderstanding 171
The Surprise of Intentional Misdirection 171
The Impact of Vivid and Imaginative Words 171
The Technique of Breaking the Fourth Wall 171
The Skill of Going Beyond the Literal 171

Final Words 173

References 175

INTRODUCTION

Have you ever admired successful individuals who seem to "have it all"? You've seen them conversing boldly at business meetings or social gatherings. They seem to have the best jobs, supportive partners, great friends, and the largest bank balances.

Stop right there! Many of them are not even smarter than you. They do not have more wisdom or education than you. They're not even prettier! So, what exactly is it? What is that secret sauce? You might assume they are simply more fortunate than you. Well, I disagree. I believe it comes down to the fact that they're merely more skilled at interacting with other people.

Nobody ever climbs to the top all by themselves. People who appear to "have it all" have won the hearts and minds of thousands of others throughout the years. That's what has helped them climb, step by step, to the top of whatever business or social ladder they choose.

Many below them may complain that they are snobs. These people feel left out and accuse influential people of being cliquish when they refuse their friendship, romance or business advances. But what those less influential or popular people may not realize is that the rejection could be because of communication blunders.

It's as if popular people have a big bag of tricks, a magic wand, or a Midas touch that transforms everything they do into a success. And they sort of do.

You're probably wondering, 'But what is this magic wand? Is there a chemical that strengthens friendships? Or is there some sort of witchcraft that wins minds, and alchemy that makes people fall in love with them?'

The answer is simple.

Those who appear to "have it all" have a few tricks up their sleeves and have honed these skills, making them winners in life's lottery. These particular skills keep people coming back for more. *The Better Relationship Guide for Work, Life, Friendships and Intimacy* teaches you the major and minor methods they use every day. So you, too, can master the game and obtain whatever you desire in life.

The majority of research in this area supports Dale Carnegie's 1936 classic *How to Win Friends & Influence People*. His timeless wisdom tells us that success can be found in smiling, expressing interest in others, and making them feel good about themselves. Thankfully, this wisdom is just as helpful today as it was eighty years ago.

So, why do we need a new book advising us how to enhance our relationships, make friends, and achieve a maximum degree of intimacy? If Dale Carnegie and so many others have already given us such useful advice, what more is there to learn today?

Two reasons.

The first: What if a wise man told you, "When in China, speak Chinese," but didn't provide you with any language lessons? Many communications specialists, like Carnegie, are like that wise old guy. They tell us what we should do but not how to do it. Plus, things have changed since Carnegie's time, and it is no longer sufficient to simply "smile" or "offer honest compliments" in today's sophisticated society.

Today's businesses tend to be more cynical, or at least cautious about who they hire, and can detect greater nuance in your smile and in your compliments. Successful or handsome individuals are often encircled by sycophants who fawn over them. And let's face it, most of us are wise to salespeople who flatter us to make a sale. Women are skeptical of suitors who tell them how beautiful they are, because they know it's usually meant to get them into bed.

The second reason: The world has changed dramatically since the 1930s, and we need a new recipe for improving ourselves and our relationships. To come up with this recipe, I examined today's superstars. I researched tactics employed by elite salespeople to complete a sale, speakers to persuade, clergy to convert, entertainers to captivate, sex icons to attract, and athletes to win.

I discovered tangible building blocks for the elusive attributes that contribute to their success. Then I boiled them down into digestible, easy-to-apply approaches and grouped them into four steps: 1) create clarity, 2) communicate effectively, 3) overcome obstacles and 4) be remarkable. I also gave each of them a name that will spring to mind immediately if you find yourself in a problematic communication situation.

As I refined these approaches, I started presenting them to audiences. The people I have worked with, many of whom were CEOs of multinational businesses, gladly shared their own perspectives. I observed the body language and facial expressions of these successful and well-liked leaders while they were in my presence. I paid close attention to their informal discussions, pace, and word choice.

I watched how they interacted with their families, friends, colleagues, and even rivals. When I discovered a hint of magic in their communication, I asked them to share it with me. We discussed it, and I then turned it into a simple little technique that others could replicate and benefit from.

This book contains my observations, as well as the insights of some of these highly productive people. Some of these insights are deceptive. Some are unexpected. But they are all attainable. Once you've mastered them, you will finally have the formula for successful work, life, friendships and intimacy.

Let's begin this exciting journey.

PART I

CREATE CLARITY

1

RELATIONSHIPS ARE INEVITABLE

The precise moment when two individuals meet has tremendous power - it is the beginning of a relationship. The first impression you make winds its way into the other person's mind and may remain with them forever.

Artists may occasionally capture this ephemeral, transitory essence. For example, a friend of mine is an exceptional caricature artist who routinely draws for many well-known magazines. He has an uncanny ability to capture not just the physical look of his subjects, but also the spirit of their character. Hundreds of celebrities' bodies and souls have been portrayed on his sketch pad. With only one look at his caricatures, you can "see" who they are.

My friend will sometimes sketch a visitor on a cocktail napkin at a party. Observers often gasp as their friend's essence appears before their eyes. He sets his pencil down and hands the napkin to the subject once he's finished and their expression is often a little puzzled. They might smile and say something like, "Thank you, that's great. But it's not really me."

But when they hear their friends around them say, "Oh yes, it is!" they're left staring back at the world's perception of themselves on a napkin.

I once asked my friend how he was able to capture people's characteristics so accurately. "It's easy," he said, "I simply stare at them."

"No, I mean how do you capture their *personalities*," I probed, "without knowing more about their lifestyle and history?"

"I told you; I simply look directly at them. Almost every aspect of someone's personality is visible from their appearance, posture, and the way they move." He motioned me over to a file where he kept his political cartoons. "See," he said, pulling out and pointing to some of the politicians he'd sketched. "Everything is in the face and body."

First impressions are permanent, and often set the course of the relationship. People's minds are whirling in this fast-paced, information-overloaded world with too many stimuli hitting us every second. We have to make rapid decisions in order to make sense of the world and move forward. As a result, every time someone meets you, they take a mental image of you. Over a long period, that picture of you becomes the data they use when interacting with you.

Is their information correct? You may be surprised to hear that it often is. Your essence already carved its way into their thoughts before your lips even parted to speak. Studies have shown that the way we appear and move accounts for more than 80 percent of other people's initial impression of us.

I've worked and lived in locations where I didn't understand the local language. When I met new people, I could immediately sense how kind they were, the amount of confidence they had, and if they were colleagues, how high up they were in the company. I could tell how influential they were simply by watching them move.

I have no psychic abilities. I don't suppose you have, either, but you could do what I do. How? Because most of us have a sixth sense about someone before we've even had a chance to develop a logical thought about them. According to research, emotional responses occur before the brain has had time to process what is triggering the reaction. As a result, the instant someone looks at you, they receive an impression, the effect of which builds the foundation for the entire relationship. My artist friend uses his sixth sense to capture that first impression.

THE CONCEPT OF CLARITY

Think of clarity as the lens through which we view everything in our lives, including our relationships. For instance, imagine gazing out a window. If the window is dirty or foggy, your view of the outside world becomes distorted. However, if it's clean and transparent, you can see everything vividly, precisely as it is.

So, let's take a moment to consider the lens through which we are viewing our own relationships. Is it foggy, clouded by past hurt or future fear, or is it clear, accurately reflecting the current reality?

The bottom line is this - if you don't know what you want, you will never get it. Clarity in relationships is about understanding exactly what you want from them. It's about setting clear, measurable goals, much like how we set targets for our careers or health.

You may be wondering how you find such clarity. Here is where the marvel of our brain comes into play, particularly the area called the **RAS,** or reticular activating system. This part of our brain is like a sophisticated search engine, filtering the vast amount of information we encounter daily and focusing on what is important to us.

By becoming clear on what we want from our relationships, we program our RAS to work in our favor. It's like entering a keyword into a search engine. Once the keyword is entered, the search engine goes to work, finding all relevant results. Similarly, once we are clear on what we want, our RAS knows what to focus on and goes to work.

This is not just a theoretical construct, but a fact backed by neuroscience. The RAS is a powerful area of our brain and understanding how it works can completely transform our relationships. As we've just discussed, the moment someone looks at you, they form an impression. But it doesn't stop there. Their RAS picks up on this impression and uses it to filter future interactions with you. So, in essence, the first impression is not just a mental image, but a data point that will influence the course of the relationship.

With this knowledge, we can better understand how paramount the role of clarity is in shaping healthy, fulfilling relationships.

WHAT ARE HUMAN RELATIONSHIPS?

As we all know, relationships are bonds formed between individuals and may be either temporary or lifelong. Social skills, such as verbal and non-verbal communication, compassion, and the capacity to listen to others, are vital to maintaining relationships.

Interaction with other people is unavoidable, so when we do not possess these skills, we struggle to cultivate relationships. Humans are social organisms by nature, and we need society and interaction with one another.

The type of connection a person has with others influences whether they feel alone or part of a community. The essence of the "social being" is tied to the interactions they are capable of forming.

Human connections are classified into two broad categories:

1. Primary relationships

These are our personal or close connections that are bound by love, compassion, or respect. For instance, romantic relationships, family relationships, and close friendships.

2. Secondary relationships

These are ties in which strong emotional feelings do not play a role but which bring people together for comfort or usefulness. Consider the interaction between a manager and a worker, or between a teacher and a student, or a patient and a doctor.

Both forms of interactions are essential and beneficial to our growth in society. Both types may coexist; for example, when a relationship begins as a secondary but evolves into a primary.

Human interactions are so vital for the evolution of life that they can help shape our existence. As a result, the strength of the ties formed is more important than the number of relationships we have.

One who shows respect, compassion, and integrity is likely to possess superior personality attributes. On the other hand, when one exhibits aggressiveness, violence, or is deceitful, they do not attract positive relationships.

Beliefs and abilities learned allow an individual to grow in accordance with their surroundings. In the workplace, for instance, particular abilities like stress management and conflict resolution are often acquired, allowing employees to overcome pressure or cope with emergency situations.

Human interactions indicate the existence or absence of values in the people involved and help us improve our quality of life in the community. Before entering into any type of relationship, we must build the skills that will enable us to engage. A healthy relationship is one where we work out our differences and maintain the relationship even when there is conflict. Such conflicts may be resolved through the growth of social skills that allow for a greater degree of understanding and genuine interest in other people.

CHARACTERISTICS OF RELATIONSHIPS

Human relationships are defined by their complexity and their diversity. The foundation of any human interaction is our desire to socialize and belong to a healthy group to preserve emotional and physical balance.

Nevertheless, depending on the context (job, religion, family, etc.), we acquire a variety of interpersonal skills.

Social psychology is the study of the interaction between the individual and the society, as well as how culture, history, politics, language, and other factors influence that interaction. This discipline investigates individual and societal behaviors, group identity, mass phenomena, and other human experiences. It explores human ties, both individually and in groups, and how certain connections affect social relationships on a larger scale.

Sociology is equally concerned with the study of human social connections but examines the ways entire groups function within society.

To understand human behavior, we need to consider the social and cultural institutions through which people are taught and trained (such as faith, family, socioeconomic class divisions, and cultural views). For example, professional, personal, and political ties all tend to intersect in the workplace. As a result, companies are becoming more committed to enhancing the work environment.

NO ONE CAN LIVE ALONE

Author John Robbins, heir to the Baskin-Robbins ice cream empire, has studied civilizations famed for their lifespan and has noted the significance of love and strong relationships in these cultures. According to Robbins, loneliness and unpleasant relationships may impair the functioning of the body's systems and contribute to ill health. "I feel that, in the end, it is love in our life that underpins and enables our greatest healing, as well as longevity."

It has been argued that loneliness, not cancer or heart disease, is the number one killer in our culture. This might come as no surprise, since loneliness is often the underlying emotion that so many try to escape through various addictions.

Those living in societies noted for their longevity do not usually live alone. People seldom lived alone before the advent of the modern world. Sadly, our civilized way of living has resulted in endemic loneliness in today's culture.

So, what happens in our minds while we're alone, and why do so many both seek and dread solitude? "The brain is constantly on," says Dr. Marcus Raichle, radiology and neurology professor at Washington University. "It's usually operating at roughly 95 percent of its full capacity." In other words, a lot is going on in the background. So what exactly is your brain doing?

In the 1990s, Raichle and his colleagues were examining the portions of the brain engaged in diverse activities. They were surprised to learn that certain areas actually start an activity when no external activities or distractions are present. These interrelated brain regions all rely on "self-referential" functions, including remembering personal experiences to guide the future, experiencing emotions, and analyzing incoming information.

The researchers dubbed these cooperating parts of the brain the "default mode network."

"When you put it all together, you realize there's something really fundamental, something to do with the idea that I have a self—me," Raichle explains. When we remove external distractions and allow our brains to roam, the default mode network is fully operational and may play a crucial part in developing our sense of identity.

Being alone might also help to relieve the mind from the spotlight effect. We tend to exaggerate the amount to which people see our successes and failures when we are in public, and when we are alone, our brains can cease believing that our activities are on full view.

In a 2003 assessment of data on the advantages of isolation, author and Associate Professor of Psychology Christopher Long noted, "Just as one's experience of seeing an artwork in a museum alters when another person steps up, our subjective experience is changed by the simplest connection with another person. We become aware of ourselves as spectators as well as the item we are witnessing." (Long, 2003)

In a 2012 *New York Times* trend item about living alone, people acknowledged adopting a range of idiosyncrasies when they no longer had roommates. These idiosyncrasies ranged from talking to the cat to singing in the shower.

But regardless of the advantages of isolation, being totally alone with our thoughts may be unpleasant or even stressful. In one trial, participants were left alone for 10 to 14 minutes with no interruptions other than an electric shock device. Surprisingly, roughly 70 percent of men and 25 percent of women preferred to give themselves shocks rather than sit with their thoughts, according to the study. In a variation of the same research, participants were instructed to spend 10 to 15 minutes alone in their homes with their thoughts. More than half admitted to cheating by standing up or distracting themselves with phones or music. Too much isolation, like many wonderful things, may be harmful. This study indicated that even moderate amounts are difficult for many people to be comfortable with.

According to another study, elderly people who are socially isolated had a 26 percent higher death risk than their socially connected peers—though the researchers suggest this is due more to the medical problems of isolation rather than the sense of loneliness. Extended solitude may increase stress and alter how the mind processes inputs.

An EEG (a device that monitors electrical activity in the brain) was used in one research study to analyze participants' responses to pleasant and unpleasant phrases, some of which had social implications such as "acceptable" and "undesirable." When socially unfavorable phrases were read out loud, lonely people's brains lit up significantly faster than other participants, indicating that their brains had evolved to pay greater attention to social risks and hazards.

The fact is, we were not designed to live alone. We are designed to live in communities with people we can turn to for affection and connection, as well as assistance when we need it. Love, communication, and support are essential for our health and happiness. Many religious orders, for instance, put a premium on silence and contemplation, but they're still organized in communities where the monks or nuns have shared lives, experiences, and companionship.

Sometimes we lack the relationship with others that we need when we don't have a loving family, community, or friends to turn to. However, before we can feel a connection with others, we must first feel connected to ourselves.

Every human being on the planet needs the sense of inner connection that comes from tuning in to their spiritual direction and from lovingly caring for themselves - physically, mentally, and spiritually. (Christopher, 2019) However, the purpose of inner connection is not to be alone. Humans fill themselves with love when they connect with themselves and their spiritual direction, and they want to share themselves with others.

We are not islands unto ourselves.

Humans need others with whom they can share their love and enjoyment of life. We need people to play and learn with. And we need someone to whom we can turn in times of despair and suffering. Without these connections, we become lonely.

Loneliness is one of the most difficult emotions to experience. As infants, we would have perished if we were left alone for too long. This is why our minds can still sense that our lives are threatened when we're alone. There are multiple ways to feel alone, including having no one in our life with whom we can express our love, and being with people who are not receptive to a connection with us.

Loneliness can be so awful that we resort to numerous addictions to escape its clutches.

Many individuals are not even aware they are lonely because they develop addictive habits to replace the feelings of loneliness. They reach for food, alcohol, drugs, or cigarettes. They may switch on the TV, find a distraction, or become angry before they are conscious of experiencing an emotion. Then, they wonder why they can't break their addictions. People might also become locked into toxic romantic relationships, unable to break away for fear of loneliness and alienation. When we are disconnected from ourselves and our spiritual direction, we may develop a connection addiction, continually seeking affirmation from others.

Continuous loneliness and inner aloneness are the result of inner disconnection and can cause a great deal of stress in the body, leading to sickness. Aside from healthy diet and exercise, one reason those in some cultures have greater lifespans than others is the constant access to love and connection with those around them.

THE BEAUTY OF COMPANIONSHIP

The reasons people become lonely may vary depending on their circumstances and surroundings. Poor health, loss of physical movement, and sensory impairments may make it difficult for someone to leave their house. Grief, living alone, and not having relatives nearby means that some people don't receive much social contact at home. Problems such as a lack of public transportation or neighborhood accessibility might also prevent people from venturing out into the community.

Companionship fulfills a core need for humans and promotes a sense of belonging. Having a companion in your daily existence, whether a family member, a caregiver, or a friend, helps keep the mind busy and minimizes social isolation. Someone to talk to, even if just for a few minutes, promotes brain stimulation and thought, and can help spark memories.

Having someone we can trust also helps us to have honest conversations about our feelings. (Christopher, 2019) Having someone to speak to about emotions, mental health, or sickness usually helps us feel less alone.

There are many paths to friendship. Companionship isn't only about having a life partner or a home full of kids. These are aspirations for many, but they aren't always attainable. Companionship takes various forms. Some may have strong ties with animals. Dogs and cats, as well as other domesticated animals, can make excellent friends. But simply seeing friendly faces, even the kind cashier at the grocery store or drug store, may provide a sense of fulfillment and camaraderie.

Lectures, community gatherings, sports events, and reading groups are all places where meaningful relationships can be cultivated. People who have the same goals, hobbies or interests are considerably more likely to bond and develop strong companionships. These interactions are much more powerful than random connections.

Companionship is a relationship consisting of empathy, love, compassion, physical touch, connection, familiarity, and a host of other positive qualities. It is not just one thing but a combination of things.

Luckily, in-person interaction isn't the only way to feel connected these days. Phone conversations, video calls, emails and texts with loved ones, friends, or colleagues can all provide similar benefits. Today's technology enables us to connect with a broader spectrum of individuals at practically any time in an affordable and easy manner.

TYPES OF RELATIONSHIPS AND THEIR EFFECTS ON YOUR LIFE

Primary and secondary relationships are divided into seven different types. They are often classified into one of many categories (though they may occasionally overlap):

- Family relationships
- Acquaintances
- Friendships
- Sexual relationships
- Romantic relationships
- Work relationships
- Situational relationships

The depth of these distinct kinds of relationships might vary greatly, and there are also many subtypes of connections within each of these fundamental categories. (Holmes, 2017) The following are some of the types of relationships we encounter in life:

Platonic relationships

A platonic relationship is a friendship that consists of a tight, personal closeness without sex or passion. These partnerships are often defined by fondness, closeness, respect, acceptance, honesty, etc. (Cherry, 2021)

Platonic relationships may take place in various contexts and can include same-sex or opposite-sex friendships. You may build a platonic relationship with a fellow student or coworker, or you might meet someone in another context, such as a club, sporting activity, or volunteer group in which you are active.

This form of connection may be really beneficial in terms of social support, which is crucial for your health and well-being. According to research, platonic friendships can help decrease risk of illness, lessen sadness or anxiety, and enhance the immune system.

Romantic relationships

Romantic relationships are defined by sentiments of love and desire for another individual. While romantic love may take many forms, it often includes emotions of infatuation, closeness, and commitment.

Experts have devised a number of different methods to explain how individuals feel and express love. Psychotherapist Robert Sternberg proposes three major components of love: desire, closeness, and decision/commitment. He defines romantic love as a blend of passion and closeness.

Romantic connections evolve over time. People often feel more passionate in the beginning of a relationship. The brain releases certain neurotransmitters (oxytocin, dopamine, and serotonin) during this infatuation stage, causing individuals to feel euphoric and "in love." (Holmes, 2017) The strength of these feelings begin to fade over time, because individuals gain higher degrees of emotional connection and understanding as their relationship progresses.

Codependent relationships

A codependent relationship is an unhealthy, dysfunctional form of relationship in which one person is emotionally, physically, or mentally dependent on the other, though both individuals may take turns alternating between caregiver and care receiver.

However, codependent relationships vary in terms of intensity. Codependency may be an aspect of various sorts of relationships, including sexual, parent-child, friendship, family member, and even work.

Casual relationships

Casual relationships are generally dating partnerships that include sex but in which there are no expectations of monogamy or commitment. Experts argue, though, that the phrase is ambiguous and may signify different things to different people.

These relationships frequently exist on a spectrum that varies in terms of frequency of contact, nature of contact, level of self-disclosure, relationship conversation, and degree of friendship. People with much more sexual experience were shown to be better able to recognize the meanings of these categories than those with less sexual experience, according to the research. (Cherry, 2021)

Young individuals often engage in casual relationships, which may have various sex-positive aspects, as long as they are characterized by communication and consent. They may fulfill the want for sex, closeness, connection, and company without the emotional and physical demands of a more committed relationship.

Open relationships

An open relationship is a sort of mutually consensual, non-monogamous partnership in which one or more parties have sex or other relationships. In an open relationship, both parties agree to have sex with other people; however, there may be restrictions or constraints. Any romantic connection, whether casual, dating, or married, may involve an open relationship.

These non-monogamous partnerships are sometimes socially frowned upon. Nonetheless, data indicates that around 21-22 percent of individuals will be engaged in some form of open relationship at some time in their lives.

Such relationships may have advantages, like enhanced sexual freedom, but they can also have drawbacks, such as jealousy or emotional suffering. But when partners create personal, emotional, and sexual boundaries, and openly express their emotions and needs to one another, open relationships can thrive.

Toxic relationships

A toxic relationship is any form of interpersonal interaction that jeopardizes or threatens your emotional, physiological, or physical well-being. Such interactions often leave us feeling embarrassed, ashamed, confused, or unsupported. Any sort of connection, including friendships, family ties, sexual partnerships, and work interactions, may be poisonous. Sometimes everyone in a relationship contributes to the poison. For example, if you are regularly nasty, critical, insecure, and pessimistic, you are almost certainly contributing to toxicity.

In other circumstances, one partner in a relationship may act in ways that elicit poisonous emotions. This may be on purpose, but in other circumstances, individuals may be unaware of how their actions influence others. They may not know any other way of behaving and talking because of their previous experiences within relationships, and this is often due to what they learned growing up.

This causes more than simply dissatisfaction; toxic relationships may be harmful to your health. Based on one research study, stress induced by unfavorable relationships, for example, has a direct influence on cardiovascular health. Feeling alienated and confused in a relationship may lead to the kind of loneliness that has been proven to harm overall health.

WHAT DOES TRUE FRIENDSHIP LOOK LIKE?

It's natural to wonder about your friendships and also what they signify to you. If you are having doubts about your friendships, a therapist may be able to help you develop stronger bonds. A therapist may assist you in improving your entire well-being with regard to relationship development, and help with feelings like social anxiety and isolation.

Do your friends often let you down? Do they constantly criticize you? Do they desert you when you need them the most? If this is the case, it may be time to redefine the term "friend." Here are some factors to consider while selecting those with whom you entrust your friendship.

A true friend always has your back

Someone who is a good friend defends you. When others attempt to injure you psychologically or physically, they will do everything in their power to keep you safe. (Cherry, 2021) They don't care who is attempting to harm you; they will protect you at any moment and in any location. If they can assist you, they will do it without hesitation or reward. A real friend is not someone who regularly shares with you unkind things other people say about you. First, they make it plain where they stand with regard to you through their words and actions. Second, they do not behave passively when others denigrate you. When it is easy and when it is not, a real friend continually supports you, both when you are there in person and when you are not.

Friends respond with empathy, understanding, and sincerity

True friends will not lie to you. They reveal their true selves. They are honest with you when it means the most. They never attempt to mislead you in order to seem stronger, more accomplished, or better than they are. A real friend goes beyond the surface because true friendship requires some level of vulnerability. When a buddy opens up to you and discusses their challenges and disappointments, it demonstrates their trust and value for you. Having a companion who trusts you with their true self is a good sign that you can do the same with them.

A genuine friend is not just truthful about themselves, but also about you. They may have unpleasant talks with you and tell you things you're reluctant to hear. The important thing is that they do it with love and grace. They do not bring you down. A good friend will push you to a level they believe your character deserves.

Regardless of differences, friends accept and embrace you for who you are

A true friend accepts you for who you are. They may motivate you to become a better version of yourself, but they can also help you appreciate who you are right now. They are not swayed by what others might say or think about you. Instead, they honor the you they've grown to know. A real friend may push you to make good choices, but they trust and appreciate your unique opinions. When you reject their advice, they don't become passive or hostile. Instead, they consider your emotions and views and respect your limits. They don't force you to become the person they want you to be. Instead, they highlight what makes you special. They support your progress and evolution. They value you for your individual style, hobbies, occupation, relationship status, and every other aspect that makes up who you are.

Friends want what is best for you

A deceptive friend may pressure you to change for them. They may tell you what you wish to hear instead of the words that would genuinely benefit you. A great friend recognizes your sentiments while also pointing you in the direction of a better, healthier existence. A real friend isn't complacent about your personal development; they don't sit back and watch you make bad decisions. They want to see you at your happiest and healthiest. They encourage you to make the decision that will lead to your desired outcome in life. They learn how to be your greatest cheerleader while still keeping you responsible for your objectives.

True friendship will never abandon you

When you're successful and happy, your true friends will be there for you. An insincere friend won't; when things become difficult for you, they move on to the next joyful, successful person. A true friend, though, remains by your side through traumas, losses, mental health problems, and physical ailments.

They do not forsake you just because it is simpler or more convenient for them to ignore you. A real friend wants to be there for you through your tough times because they genuinely care about you. (Cherry, 2021)

A friend isn't only there for the things you have in your life – they're there for you! As life becomes more difficult and you find yourself feeling sad or burdened, you won't have to face these obstacles alone when you have a real friend in your corner.

2

PEOPLE ARE COMPLICATED

Many of us are familiar with the old joke some comedians tell when they walk on stage and ask, "Well, how do you like me so far?" But why does this resonate with audiences and cause them to laugh? Because we all ask the same question about ourselves. We know, unconsciously or consciously, how others respond to us when we meet them. Do they give us a certain look? Do they grin? Do they tilt their head in our direction? These are the ones who appreciate how precious and unique we are and they are appealing to us. They have excellent taste. On the other hand, do they turn away, clearly underwhelmed by our majesty? These are the idiots!

Two individuals who are getting to know one other are like pups smelling each other. We don't have wagging tails or bristly hair, but we do have the ability to narrow or widen our eyes. We have hands that flash their knuckles or soften unconsciously in the palms-up "I surrender" position. There are hundreds of additional spontaneous responses that occur in the initial few seconds of meeting someone.

Attorneys who conduct *voir dire* – the process of selecting potential jury members for a trial - are aware of this. They pay special attention to the physical responses of those they interview. They watch body language, listen to voice intonation and make mental notes of facial expressions.

Body language is actually fascinating to learn about. Palms up, slightly open, indicates approval. (Gurteen, 2022) Making a fist often indicates rejection of the particular topic being discussed. Maintaining or losing eye contact while discussing their opinions on large awards for damages or the death sentence can tell attorneys a great deal about which way a potential juror will lean. Some lawyers even call in a jury consultant, who sits on the sidelines and meticulously records every twitch, giving their recommendations afterwards.

It may not be a surprise to many that trial attorneys often hire women to conduct these observations, because females are usually better than males at reading body language. Women tend to be more emotionally sensitive than men, often noticing subtle changes in their partner's disposition and asking things like, "Is there something upsetting you, honey?"

Body language is important and sometimes hotly debated, especially in trials. During the famous Chicago Seven trial of 1969, defense counsel William Kunstler submitted a formal complaint about the judge's physical movements. During the prosecution's conclusion, the judge leaned back, thus, Kunstler argued, signaling to the jury that he was interested. Others, however, argued that the gesture was more likely a demonstration of apathy.

The judgments of advocates, legal counselors, jurors, and witnesses continue to be heavily influenced today by non-verbal signals. Body language in courts has a subtle impact on most criminal proceedings. Every participant in a courtroom is continually sending and watching gestures and facial expressions. The defense and prosecuting attorneys both use gestures and body language in their arguments to persuade the jury and the court that they're correct. Witnesses often send more information through their body language than through their testimony. Attorneys use various methods to establish a rapport with the jurors, even when they have little information about them.

Just as in the attorney/juror scenario, when building a rapport with anyone, it's important to use "warm" non-verbal actions (such as close distance, eye contact, smiles, and a soft tone of voice) while avoiding adversarial aspects (sarcastic tone, scowling or frowning, etc.). There is a great deal of evidence that rapport is associated with the adoption of 'mirroring,' which is exactly what it sounds like: mirroring the other person's speech style, facial expressions, or movements.

Credibility is a mixture of exhibiting competence, trust, friendliness, energy, character, and social abilities. According to research, speakers are more believable when they speak fluently while maintaining eye contact, use intense facial expressions, and gesture freely but without stress.

But why do we put forth so much effort into figuring out other people? Because people are very complex beings.

WHY ARE PEOPLE SO COMPLICATED?

The human body has roughly 37 trillion cells and approximately 200 different kinds of cells. The human brain is the most complicated mechanism known to science. It is a very interconnected structure. Estimates vary, but the human brain is thought to have roughly 86 billion neurons. In addition, every neuron in the brain may be linked to up to 10,000 additional neurons, with up to 100 trillion synaptic connections.

We are immensely complicated, dynamic, unpredictable, passionate, and sometimes illogical beings with cognitive biases.

There is nothing more complicated than a human.

Everything in a relationship is subjective. How could it not be when so many elements influence our views? Things like how we were raised, the genes we inherited, and the surroundings we've been exposed to all influence how we perceive individuals who cross our path.

Given these many variables, your assessment of someone may be utterly at variance with someone else's—someone whose biological and past experience differs significantly from your own. Whether it's a question of comprehension, perception, or judgment, it's important to recognize that we all live in a world where subjectivity reigns supreme. And that the certainty you may have about another's motivations and actions may be the opposite of how someone else feels.

There are many examples of this phenomenon that pertain not just to how we—as opposed to others—react to a certain individual, but also to our perspectives on everything under the sun. (Buckley, 2022) For example, is it justified to sentence someone to death as a kind of retributive justice? Or is it never justified since the death penalty could be considered vindictive? Such topics like "merciful" or "compassionate" judgment are even more complicated. For example, suppose conditions indicate that a criminal's behavior was more coerced than chosen. How ethical is it to exact vengeance on someone whose bad deed may have been less knowingly evil and more naively wrongheaded? What if their genetic makeup, along with the erroneous lessons they absorbed as children about themselves and the world, made it very difficult for them to police themselves? What if they (like the rest of us) were "programmed" or dictated to? How much free will do they have?

Can people, who are so varied in so many ways, ever agree on what constitutes non-volitional behavior, or whether such activity should be penalized at all?

Let's return to the intricacies of human action and the inherent arbitrariness, or subjectivity, in assessing another's action. It makes little difference whether one position is starkly opposite to another or complementary to it, because each viewpoint is personally significant or "genuine." They all have their own (subjective) legitimacy. Each is founded on the individual's experience and their often-predetermined perception.

To make matters even more confusing, morality—or "proper" behavior—is mostly determined by one's society. And various cultures and civilizations have always had varied ideas about what is acceptable or deserving of approval. So how are we to judge what's virtuous and what's wicked behavior?

How much of the behavior is "rooted" in one's culture—the area and people to whom one belongs? Given this additional complicating factor, who has ultimate power to assess another's behavior? It would be wonderful to say that we simply need to evaluate the facts. Unfortunately, the facts alone may be open to unlimited interpretation. (Buckley, 2022)

How we see people is determined by our point of view, which is influenced by genetic inheritance, familial upbringing, and a variety of contextual factors. So, given how diverse and undeniably subjective all points of view are, what does this imply about how to effectively live in the world?

Many people turn to religion and the concept of superior, compassionate deities to help them make sense of this enormous complexity—and the existential perplexity that may come with it. Humans often choose to put their trust in a higher power that can lead them through such a quagmire. But I would suggest that this dilemma is best handled through careful application, and expansion, of the golden rule.

THE ROLE THAT TEMPERAMENT PLAYS IN A PERSON

One of the wonderful things about humankind is that every single person is unique. Your sister may be laid-back or easygoing, but your mother may be high-strung and nervous. Maybe you're quick to fight, easy to please, or a little gloomier than your friends.

These personality traits determine your temperament, which refers to biological distinctions that influence behavior or emotional reaction to stimuli, particularly in a psychological sense. The temperament is the psychological and emotional framework that defines a person. (Buckley, 2022) This biological wiring is often set at birth; calm newborns frequently develop into calm adults, and vice versa.

Certainly most of us are capable of experiencing the whole spectrum of human emotions. You will have both joyful and sad days, despite your temperament. Whenever a loved one dies, you will experience sadness and grief. If you are under stress at work or school, you may become irritable. The intensity and relevance of your response to setbacks and accomplishments are determined by your temperament.

Temperament may also influence your proclivity to mental illness. According to research, intrinsic characteristics have a direct role in the development of mental diseases. For example, it has been discovered that "negative affect," or a pessimistic perspective of oneself and one's environment, might predispose one to a broad range of mental diseases. (Buckley, 2022) Similarly, "poor effortful control," or the inability to manage behaviors and emotional reactions in youngsters, may result in antisocial personality disorder.

Many mental health professionals divide personality and temperament into "Big Five" characteristics: openness, conscientiousness, extraversion, agreeableness, and neuroticism. Some, though, split it even further. The Center for Early Childhood Mental Health Consultation, run by Georgetown University, is intended for children, but its simple categorizations might provide an intriguing method to examine our own personality. They categorize the most frequent temperaments as follows:

- Level of activity: Would you rather shoot hoops or relax on a hammock?
- Distractibility: How great are you at concentrating – do you prefer to zone out?
- Intensity: Are you normally calm, or do you react violently to bad or happy news?
- Regularity: Is your routine consistent, or does it change on a daily basis?
- Sensitivity: How sensitive are you to external stimuli like bright lights or irritating clothing?
- Approachability: Do you like traveling and meeting new people, or do you prefer to stay at home?
- Adaptability: How do you deal with change?
- Persistence: How long will you try when things become difficult?
- Mood: Are you normally upbeat or downcast?

As you can see, "temperament" encompasses much more than mood. It examines all of the little parts that, when put together, form you — and your mental health. Each aspect is represented by a spectrum. You aren't "regular" or "irregular," "energetic," or "lazy." We are all unique.

Let's assume you're a rather intense person who is prone to melancholy. (Buckley, 2022) You could be prone to depression: after all, your glass is usually half-empty, and you take defeats personally. It's easy to understand how these personality characteristics might contribute to depression, particularly if they spiral out of control.

WE ALL HAVE DIFFERENT TEMPERAMENTS

Psychologists believe there are four temperament types, the names of which date back to ancient Greek medicine. Most of us almost certainly possess both main and secondary temperament types. A personality may be made up of any mix of temperament types. The descriptions below are merely a summary of qualities that those with certain temperaments may display; they are not an exhaustive or diagnostic list. Many individuals will match with a combination of them or with specific features of the descriptions.

MEET THE MELANCHOLY HUMAN

Most of us associate sadness with depression. But the melancholic temperament type is cautious rather than dejected. Melancholy temperaments are precision and quality-oriented, and tend to stress over knowing what is proper. They may be seen as perfectionists due to their meticulous attention to detail.

Characteristics

The melancholic disposition follows the rules. They may be cautious and apprehensive in strange situations, yet when confronted with an unpleasant scenario, they can become aggressive. They are reserved and introverted. This personality type is factual, rational, and analytical. To perform optimally, these folks must have a firm action plan and stick to it.

Those with a melancholic disposition may experience anxiety. They may be concerned about the future and what others think of them. They also worry about how things may have been done differently in the past. As a result, they tend to be resistant to living in the moment.

Even if their lives become cluttered, people with this disposition are often highly organized. They arrive on time for meetings and expect others to do the same. They'll collect as much information as necessary and ask detailed questions before reaching a conclusion.

Melancholy personalities will not trust people unless they are certain of their intentions. They have a tough time forming connections, and have high expectations for their relationships.

SANGUINE

People with sanguine temperaments are generally people-oriented and extroverted. They work well with others and strive to do good for one another, and are generally helpful. This is the most common temperament type and can be either main or secondary. It is equally common in both men and women. Some individuals are labeled "hyper sanguine" because they're so chatty and energetic that they can be exhausting to be around.

Characteristics

Individuals with a sanguine temperament exhibit a broad variety of emotions and behaviors. They are the most adaptable of the temperaments. They're able to participate in almost any human activity, and like instances when they can engage with or influence their surroundings.

Individuals with a sanguine temperament are spontaneous and playful. They are always on the go and usually upbeat. They have a great sense of humor, are amusing, and readily entertained. They are very loving, trustworthy and expressive, and quickly form connections.

When you meet someone with a sanguine temperament, you will probably feel like you have been friends for a while. They are easy to talk with and get to know. They are highly gregarious, chatty, and welcoming. They often become engrossed in conversation and lose track of time. However, if they become bored, they might swiftly lose interest. Their attention is directly proportional to how much they love the discussion or activity.

Those with a sanguine temperament lack a filter, so when they believe or feel something, they will simply come right out and say it. Their excitement for life often leads to forgetfulness and disorganization. They can also be very competitive, and are dominant in athletics, politics, and business. They worry about creating a poor first impression and being rejected. They want to be accepted, but they also want to be the best they can be.

PHLEGMATICS

Phlegmatic temperaments are almost diametrically opposed to sanguine temperaments. They are service-oriented, with introverted personality features, yet will collaborate with others to reach a shared purpose. (Buckley, 2022) These individuals may seem inert and lack overall desire or ambition to achieve a goal or milestone. However, it is possible to be predominantly sanguine and secondarily phlegmatic, or the other way around.

Characteristics

The phlegmatic temperament's passiveness is exhibited in a particular set of features. They are uncomplicated, peaceful, and somewhat emotionless. They may be indecisive but are pleasant, and they are typically content to let others make choices for them.

People with a phlegmatic temperament are hesitant to warm up to others, yet they readily establish friends. Because they are so amiable and patient, they are one of the simplest temperament types to get along with. They keep to their habits and are resistant to change.

Phlegmatics lead tranquil lives focused on home and family, and have little interest in those outside their circle. They are devoted to their friends, and will remain in a relationship regardless of what the other individual does or says. However, after a relationship has ended, they are unlikely to return.

This personality type is willing to let things happen on their own. They are not quick to make judgments, but as noted earlier, they tend to lack ambition. They are resistant to change and may need a significant amount of time to adjust when change is forced on them.

CHOLERICS

The choleric temperament is the least common of the four types. Those with a choleric temperament are goal-oriented, setting objectives and adhering to them until they're met. As a result, they have an optimistic attitude and are always pushing ahead. Regardless of the obstacles, they approach everything with the aim of attaining their goals. The choleric temperament is more prevalent as a secondary temperament, albeit not as frequent as other combinations.

Characteristics

People with choleric temperaments are outgoing and self-assured. They are self-sufficient and determined. They have sharp brains and are often energetic and practical. Their style of communication is aggressive and straightforward, and they are often curt to the point of rudeness.

This disposition type likes taking chances and is often bored. They can be arrogant and opinionated, finding it easy to make choices, not just for themselves but for others. In relationships, they might be quite domineering. (Buckley, 2022) It's no surprise that cholerics tend to sleep less than other temperaments.

People with choleric temperaments are imaginative. They seem to never run out of ideas or goals, all of which are usually feasible. They are firm in their beliefs, though, and will not yield to peer pressure.

While those with this disposition might be empathetic and can mobilize for social issues, they are slow to form intimate ties. Even though they're not hesitant to meet new people, they are likely to have only a few close friends, as they have a hard time empathizing with others. They are, however, slow to anger, despite the fact that their dominant personality and direct method of communicating might be misinterpreted as angry.

HOW TO ADAPT TO DIFFERENT HUMANS WITH DIFFERENT TEMPERAMENTS

When we observe that someone communicates or behaves differently from us, it's easy to become upset and describe them as "difficult" or "annoying." Some people are more introverted, preferring to remain quiet and think things through on their own. Others are more outgoing, preferring to be louder and more social. Some are born leaders, while others want to be led. It can be helpful to spend some time considering the differences in our own personality and try to avoid labeling.

Different cultures interact and communicate in different ways, which may lead to cross-cultural misreadings. Making a joke at the expense of another person can be a way for some to exhibit camaraderie, but others may deem it improper, which can lead to feelings of bullying.

Those from Western cultures generally want to be told things clearly and may perceive a person to be untrustworthy if they do not speak with them in a direct manner. In many other cultures, though, direct communication is considered disrespectful and inconsiderate. Even when two individuals are doing their best, their differing cultural viewpoints could lead to misunderstandings.

Instead of thinking, "I like this about so-and-so, but I don't like it when they do this or say that," attempt to de-personalize your sentiments and accept people as they are. When individuals behave in ways we don't like, we might become angry and frustrated because we judge them based on our personal preferences. Perceiving individuals objectively, as in "Tom is simply Tom, and I don't need to have an idea about that," might make it easier to let go and accept someone as they are.

We may shun those with viewpoints that are not our own. Try the above technique and consider why someone might have a different point of view or method of operation than you. When we consider the distinctions good rather than negative, different personality types may challenge and expand our own patterns of thinking and doing.

When differences seem to be too great, focusing on a shared purpose or objective might help bring individuals together. A group might have various points of view, histories, and communication styles, but they are all working toward the same objective in the workplace: getting the job done. It's beneficial to everyone to focus on the work at hand rather than the disparities between the members.

Respecting oneself does not always entail taking a hardline approach and sticking to your guns. It's often necessary to know how to pick our fights. Letting go of minor disagreements allows us to focus on completing a task without adding additional stress.

When you find yourself in a situation where you have trouble communicating with someone, try changing your interaction style to match theirs. If they have an introverted personality, make an attempt to converse with them one-on-one rather than in a group environment. If they're more outgoing, engage with them in a group setting and ensure they can express their thoughts with others.

Not only do our character traits and cultural origins impact us, but so do our moods and emotions. Even though we strive to keep our job and personal lives separate, we are all individuals and we have experiences that impact our overall attitude. It's important to remember that we don't know what someone else is going through inside and that we all need a little tolerance from time to time.

DETERMINE A PERSON'S TEMPERAMENT JUST BY ASKING THEM A FEW QUESTIONS

1. Can you describe yourself?

This question may seem deceptive at first. But you're not asking "What's your personality like?" or "What do the majority of people think about you?" You're not asking someone to characterize themselves physically, professionally, emotionally, or in any other manner, but instead giving them leeway to decide what to tell you about themselves. Pay attention to the characteristics they choose to share first, as well as their choice of words. Shy or timid individuals choose adjectives like "observant" while extroverted people use phrases like "athletic."

2. Can you tell me about your biggest achievement?

This one provides one key piece of information about a person's background while also revealing two subtle aspects of their personality. First, it reveals their primary interests; again, the question is vague; do they react with a career or a personal accomplishment?

Also, how recently did this feat occur? How do they behave while bringing it up? How long did it take them to think of it? If this "accomplishment" is shared only after a lengthy pause, it might indicate that they had many or few previous achievements. You'll have to dig a little further to find out.

3. Have you recently bought or read any good books?

The responses you'll receive here will vary greatly. First, distinguish between readers and non-readers. Some people may say, "I don't read books," but more often than not, non-readers will pause for a long time, and then they'll mention a classic school or college work.

Popular book readers, business and self-help readers, literary aficionados, pop science devotees, and a variety of other types may all be identified.

4. What is your ideal job?

The more open-ended the question, the better. Rather than "Where do you see yourself in five years?" ask, "What is your ideal job?" In a job interview, a person will likely describe the position for which they're applying. Others may emphasize artistic endeavors. Others will describe occupations that do not exist (or are highly uncommon), such as "beer taster" or "dog cuddler."

Whatever reaction you get will tell you how much thought this person has given the idea.

5. Who most inspires you?

This question will provide you with more detailed and insightful information on the other person. Your subject might mention a family member or someone they know in their life, but people can also respect an athlete or pop culture star, while others might admire successful businesspeople.

The answer could help you discover something about the person you're speaking with, their IQ or age, but more significantly, about their beliefs. What distinguishes their "hero" from everyone else?

Admittedly, some of these questions are a bit too direct to ask random individuals on the street, but after you've warmed up to a new acquaintance, feel free to ask them. How people react, respond, and word their responses will reveal a lot about the sort of person in front of you.

Living Peacefully with People Takes Understanding and Acceptance

If we wish to have inner calm with everyone around us, we must recognize that we exist to assist and love others, not to exert control over them. Trying to manipulate others and compel them to adopt our point of view is a surefire way to damage our inner peace, as well as theirs.

We must first comprehend people from their perspective if we want them to understand us. When we attempt to exert too much control over others, any connection we have may collapse.

Tolerance is often all that is required to bring about peace; when things go wrong, this quality will make all the difference. Compassion for others entails respecting variety and being prepared to 'live and let live.' When things grow heated and people lose their patience, it may lead to anger, sadness, prejudice, even violence. Humans fight with one another because they no longer tolerate one another. It is often best to simply walk away from a heated situation.

When we are angry or attempting to win an argument, we tend to lose our senses and all we're doing is trying to convince the other side that we are correct. But this is not productive for anyone. Instead, take a break, go have a bite to eat, find a distraction. When our mood changes, so does our thinking. All of a sudden, we might uncover fresh answers and begin to grasp 'the other side.'

Learning to live in the now is one of the most effective methods for living in harmony with yourself and with others. When we live in the present moment, we are in a state of awareness in which we are not our ideas but rather the observer who's watching how our ideas flow. This is a higher level of self-awareness that many strive for. When we live in the present, we can see the broader picture and discover fresh perspectives on the challenges and hurdles we encounter in life.

The truth is, comparing ourselves to others is the quickest way to lose our serenity and joy. While comparison may foster competitiveness and growth, too many of us blindly compare everything in our life to that of others' lives. We may see a friend with a new car and decide we want one too. Maybe someone we know has a larger home or takes regular exotic vacations, and we envy them and find ourselves comparing our homes and recreational life to theirs.

Accepting other people as they are is an effective method to find harmony. Ultimately, we cannot transform others, and we cannot force them to be or behave like us. Everyone is unique, and everyone thinks in their own manner. When we attempt to change others, we lose our inner calm, and this leads to arguments and resentments. Choose to accept and embrace others for who they are and understand them from their perspective.

Another one of the most important aspects of finding success in life is accepting responsibility for all that happens in your life.

When we accept responsibility, we gain control.

When you are in charge, you will be at ease because you recognize that everything happens as a result of your own choosing. And when you accept responsibility, you have the ability to change. For example, if your company fails, you might choose to blame the industry, your customer, your staff, or some other factor. But if you accept responsibility and recognize that your choices helped to bring you to where you are, you'll feel empowered. When we are accountable, we are in charge; we can adjust, improve, and do things differently, and, most significantly, we find peace, both inside ourself and with others.

Finally, no one can make you feel less than you are until you give them permission. No one can make you unhappy, angry, or frustrated unless you surrender to them in the first place. Take charge of your life and you will discover serenity.

We all need to define what we want in our relationships. We must set relationship objectives and goals. Luckily for you, the next chapter is all about defining yourself and your relationship goals. Let's continue our journey to better relationships!

3

DEFINING WHAT YOU WANT

Why should you read this book to learn how to construct good relationships with people? Why not learn from the best friend-winner the world has ever known? You could run into them in the street tomorrow. When you approach them, they'll start wagging their tail. They will leap with joy if you stop and pet them. And even better, there are no hidden intentions behind their displays of affection: they don't want to sell you anything or date you.

That's right, I'm talking about a dog. When I was five years old, my father brought home a small yellow-haired puppy. He was the pleasure and light of my childhood. Every afternoon around four-thirty, he would lay in the front yard, his lovely eyes fixed on the path, and as soon as he heard my voice or saw me, he would race eagerly up the hill to greet me, jumping and barking ecstatically.

His name was Tuff, and he could make more friends in thirty days by being truly curious about others than a human could make in two years by trying to get others interested in them. Much like the human's best friend, if we show interest in others, we can make more friends in a mere two months than we could make in two years of trying to persuade others to like us.

We all know people who spend way too much time trying to get others interested in them. Of course, it doesn't work. People are mostly preoccupied with themselves for much of the time. It's just the way human beings are; we're the central figures in our own dramas. Think about it - which image do you search for first when you're looking at a group photo in which you're included?

We will never have many honest, sincere friends if we strive only to impress others and pique their interest in us. This is not how true friends are created.

In his book, *What Life Could Mean to You,* Austrian psychotherapist and founder of the school of individual psychology, Alfred Adler, said, "It is the man who is not involved with his fellow men who has the most problems in life and does the greatest harm to others. All human failures stem from such individuals."

However, before taking a sincere interest in someone, we need to define what we want from them.

TAKING INTEREST IN OTHER PEOPLE

When you are truly interested in another person, you will create strong connections. People can usually sense if your interest is genuine or self-serving, so if you only pretend to be interested, you'll be quickly rejected. (Parienti, 2020) Show genuine interest and care for the person, and they will gladly accept you.

To demonstrate your interest in someone, give them your undivided attention. Learning about their interests, objectives, points of view, and worries will strengthen ties. The more you know about other people, the easier it is to develop rapport. As we will discuss in this chapter, discovering common ground with others makes it easier to achieve mutually satisfactory outcomes.

APPROACH RELATIONSHIPS WITH CLEAR INTENTIONS

Clear intentions in a relationship are not always objectives or goals but rather aspirations, anticipations, and even a dream that you hope for as the partnership evolves. Once you've decided that you've met someone you want to spend more time with, you'll need to talk about what your objectives are in this connection to see where each of you stands.

But before we can freely and totally love someone else with purpose, we must possess a certain amount of self-love. Confidence, uniqueness, and independence all help us share ourselves with another person without relying on them.

Good and clear intentions in a relationship are achievements that you and your partner pledge to attain as the relationship evolves. A union can only be successful if both individuals work together to maintain it. It requires significant work to sustain desire, cultivate love and respect, and create closeness, not just in the beginning but throughout your life together.

When a partner brings certain elements into a relationship, this indicates they have good intentions. Such elements might include:

- Being courteous and respectful
- Offering unconditional love

- Engaging in honest, vulnerable dialogue
- Sharing feelings of passion, love, and closeness
- Showing encouragement and gratitude
- Expressing admiration and offering compliments
- Avoiding criticism and complaints
- Guaranteeing personal space
- Accepting and forgiving when there is disagreement

Remember that it takes two individuals to work together; each person must have good intentions.

How do we establish goals?

Expression is key!

When we first meet someone, many of us put on airs instead of introducing our true selves. Instead of paying attention to what's going on and really listening to the other person, we find ourselves preoccupied with perfecting our own performance. To avoid this behavior, we must make a real effort to show ourselves truthfully so the other person can quickly determine whether they have a genuine connection with us. Instinct does not deceive.

Take the initiative with confidence

Set goals in a friendship that will lead you to feel safe with the other person. When you have conviction, it helps the other person to offer equivalent strength by disclosing their characteristics and what they want from the relationship.

Everything should be smooth

The goal of a successful relationship is minimal or no conflict. When you think about each connection in your life, do you accept or suffer inconveniences or difficulties? Why do you accept conflict with someone you spend time with?

A good relationship should be simple, straightforward, and uncomplicated. That is not to suggest that there will never be obstacles or hurdles. Of course, this is part of having a loving, long-term connection. Life happens, but fighting with your partner is rarely productive or beneficial.

Mistakes are unavoidable

Those in a loving relationship never condemn or hold each other accountable for making mistakes over and over again. (Sasson, 2021) Mistakes are discussed, worked through, appropriately apologized for, and forgiven. Following that, there is an intention that what occurred will not occur again.

Individualism is preserved and expected

When we marry, we do not instantly become one person with our partner - that is not the purpose. Instead, we maintain our uniqueness. Retaining our own hobbies, interests, friends, and allowing the other their personal space is as crucial as spending quality time together.

Be patient with your intentions

Even though both parties' aim is clear from the start, there is no rush to progress the partnership toward a defined "goal." Before committing further, it is critical to completely understand the attributes of one another, ensure that your motives are genuine, and determine if the connection is real. If you believe that things are becoming stagnant or that one of you is hesitating, take some time to consider what's really going on.

Vulnerability is not a bad thing

Vulnerability between two individuals creates a stronger link and pulls the relationship closer together. You may need to demonstrate your understanding of your mate's objectives by leading the way with deeper talks. These can help disclose who you are and build a level of trust and comfort so the other person will be more willing to be open up, as well.

WHAT ARE YOUR GOALS FOR DIFFERENT RELATIONSHIPS?

What are your relationship's objectives? The phrase "relationship objectives" has recently become somewhat of a social media fad. Suddenly, the internet is filled with some over-the-top, some lovely, some odd, some comical, and some exaggerated ideals of what a couple or friendship should strive for. But all this hoopla nevertheless raises the very valid question: what should you ignore, and what are the true relationship objectives you desire in your life?

The goal, at its most fundamental, is an ideal, value, lesson, or experience to strive for. It should be inspiring rather than unreachable. Relationship objectives should be considered as a rough guideline for how to effectively offer and receive love, nothing more or less. In this chapter, I discuss all types of relationships, although I am mainly focused on the romantic partnership.

Your relationship objectives should be based on reality rather than fiction. Many public partnerships, from friendships to romantic partners, have been immortalized in the media, but the fairytale image is rarely accurate or real. In the following paragraphs, we break down actual relationship objectives to commit to, long-term connection goals to construct, and offer a list of relationship goals for happiness.

You can create happier, stronger, and improved relationships if you:

Accept imperfection.

One of the most fundamental but sometimes forgotten relationship objectives is that no relationship is flawless. You are not flawless, and neither is the person in front of you. You are both flawed individuals who love each other and have decided to share your lives. In movies, fictional stories, and especially on social media, relationships are often portrayed as perfect, or without flaws. But a good, healthy relationship is never without some strife. Try not to compare your relationship to anyone else's, particularly one created for entertainment purposes, and be more realistic about your own and your partner's flaws.

Have mutual understanding.

Everyone has distinct relationship objectives and preferences for how they express and receive love. This is where understanding your love language comes in. The five love languages were developed by Gary Chapman, Ph.D., and include words of affirmation, social time, receiving presents, acts of charity, and physical contact. Understanding your language, as well as your partner's language, will likely help you both better understand and support one another.

Be consistent in your essential ideals and views.

Making sure you and the other person have the same underlying values and views should be central to your relationship objectives. This is not a one-time talk, but rather one that will continue as your situation changes and you mature as people. Let's imagine that five years ago, the ability to pick up and move whenever you wished was a key value for both of you. But now you're looking for stability and want to settle down. It is critical that you discuss how your values may have evolved so that you can determine how to move forward together.

Enhance communication.

Everyone enters a love partnership with a unique background, worldview, talents, and shortcomings. Do not start thinking about how the other person feels about a certain subject. It is far better if you ask them about their feelings and thoughts. Your mutual objectives should include always improving your communication with each other, which is essential for a strong relationship.

Establish a judgment-free zone.

Nobody enjoys being chastised, particularly when they are discussing something difficult with their partner. Creating a judgment-free zone will help the other person feel comfortable and to be honest and open with you. If you are irritated and unsure about your ability to remain neutral, find a method to take a break and restart an unpleasant conversation once you are calmer. While unpleasant talks are never easy, they are vital if you want to build your relationship over time.

Maintain emotional control.

Your partner is not a mind reader. It is up to each individual to effectively explain their requirements to the other person. For instance, if your partner said something that irritated you, instead of becoming quiet, blowing up, or calling them names, simply say, "That hurt my feelings." Focusing on how what the other person did or said made you feel is a true relationship aim that can be extremely beneficial.

Be open to criticism.

It might be frightening to be vulnerable at first, but being able to express ourselves is the cornerstone of a happy and healthy connection. Every relationship has good and bad days. How you support one other on tough days will reveal your long-term sustainability. It's critical that you both feel unconditionally accepted and that neither of you feels the need to suppress your emotions for any reason.

Put each other first.

It's especially crucial as time passes to remember to prioritize each other, especially in a romantic relationship. With our hectic schedules and lifestyles, it's tempting to put a long-term relationship on the back burner. However, continuous affection and care should always be included in shared objectives. Making an effort is necessary for a strong long-term connection.

Work together against a storm.

A loved one dies, a child becomes ill, your partner is laid off, you are in an accident — being in a partnership means you are committed to facing problems together. When things are going well, it's easy to be there for each other. The ultimate measure of a strong relationship is if you can be there for each other when times are tough. If your partner is having a difficult time, think about how you can best help them. And if you are the one working through a challenge, be sure to explain your needs to the other person so they understand them. Remember, they are not a mind reader!

Show mutual respect.

You may not like everything the other person says or does, but it's important that you respect them. When we're able to say something like, "I don't particularly agree with you, but I appreciate your perspective," we're telling our partner that our relationship is stable enough for each of us to have our own unique point of view. If you are constantly feeling disrespected by your mate, it may be time to seek other helpful aids.

WHY YOU MUST DEFINE YOUR RELATIONSHIPS WITH OTHERS

We've all likely heard the saying, "It is what it is," but when we're in a relationship with someone and it's not exclusive, there are all sorts of terms to describe the situation. Lovers, Open Relationship, Friends with Benefits, Casual Dating, etc. And when we're seeing someone exclusively, these terms are Boyfriend, Girlfriend, Partner, Significant Other, etc.

Defining the connection is a vital step in ensuring that the person we're with sees the relationship the same way we do. Clarity isn't about pressing the other person to commit; rather, it's about ensuring that both parties know what the relationship is and isn't.

Even in a casual chat, avoiding a label generally signals dishonesty. The concept of "Let's not put a label on it" enables one person to name it anything they want at the moment - exclusive, informal, a priority, not a priority — while leaving the other person in the dark to draw their own conclusions. It's neither honest nor nice. "It is what it is" becomes meaningless if one member of the relationship is unaware of what on earth "is" actually means.

It might also be disingenuous simply because one person is afraid to say what they want for fear of the other not being in agreement with them. By leaving things vague, they can always claim it was a miscommunication rather than acknowledging they were being purposely misleading. This may also extend one person's advantage over the other, which is unhealthy.

It could also signify a relational imbalance in which one person has complete control over the outcome while the other anxiously or impatiently awaits a definition. Continuing to insist on avoiding definitions offers one person complete authority while giving the other person none. It does not imply equality or health in the partnership. A simple discussion should not result in the avoidance or dismissal of someone's concerns. A connection does not cease to exist just because it is not referred to as such. It merely makes navigation more difficult.

This imbalance is often caused by immaturity. The inability to communicate may not be malicious, yet it may still cause damage. Avoiding a definition might be a dead giveaway that a person isn't ready for any type of partnership.

In addition to identifying our present connections, we must characterize our prior ones, as well. Labeling a connection is crucial not merely for when we're trying to figure out the ground rules and where it's heading, but also so we have a better understanding of our own experiences. For example, avoiding labeling an abusive relationship as abusive would not alter what it was, but it may postpone our recovery from it.

Being able to discuss what our relationships are and aren't is an important characteristic of being a well-adjusted, functional adult capable of connecting with others. There is no pressure. It's just a matter of being mature enough to call things what they are without evasion.

It also assists us in healing and gaining perspective. It's too simple to tell ourselves a tale through rose-colored glasses, to convince ourselves that someone who refuses to define a connection means well and that we must both be on the same page. Or to convince ourselves that a previous relationship wasn't all that horrible. But if we can gain perspective on our connections and then identify them, we might find it easier to manage our interactions.

Words have tremendous power. Foe and friend are opposite labels. Dating and becoming a partner are two different things. Unhealthy and abusive are distinct things. Naming things doesn't alter what they are; it only affects how we interact with them.

DEFINING WHAT YOUR RELATIONSHIPS WITH COWORKERS WILL LOOK LIKE

Humans are sociable animals by nature. And, given that we invest one-third of our lives at work, it's obvious that having strong connections with our coworkers can make our work life more pleasurable. The more at ease coworkers are with one another, the more secure they will feel sharing their thoughts, brainstorming, and accepting fresh concepts. This degree of collaboration is required to embrace change, develop, and innovate. When employees experience the benefits of working together in this manner, group enthusiasm and productivity skyrocket.

Good working connections also provide us with freedom. Instead of wasting time and energy coping with unpleasant connections, we may concentrate on possibilities ranging from new business to personal growth. Establishing a powerful professional network can help you advance your career, offering you chances that you might otherwise miss.

Self-awareness, trust, respect, open communication, and inclusiveness are all required for a good professional relationship. Let's elaborate a little more.

You can be honest and open in your ideas and actions when you trust your team members. And you won't have to spend time or energy "watching your back."

Respect is among the most important elements. Respectful colleagues recognize contributions of others and create solutions established on joint wisdom, knowledge, and creativity.

Self-awareness allows us to take responsibility for our statements and behavior, and prevents us from allowing bad feelings to affect those around us.

Inclusion means welcoming varied individuals and viewpoints. Even when coworkers disagree with us, it's important to include their ideas and perspectives in our decision-making.

All good relationships are founded on open, honest communication. The more successfully you interact with individuals around you, whether via emails or instant messages, face-to-face meetings, or video chats, the better you'll connect.

DEFINING YOUR RELATIONSHIP WITH YOUR FAMILY AND RELATIVES

As most of us know, strong families are essential to our culture. Our family lets us know how to live in the real world. A strong family loves and cares for all of its members and provides them with whatever they need to get through life's most difficult times.

Strong families communicate well.

Strong families communicate openly, so all members feel heard and appreciated. Improving your active listening skills and those of your family members is one of the most effective methods of building a solid family dynamic. We can't create good connections unless we can hear each other.

Actively listen to each other to strengthen family bonds.

Give your family members your undivided attention; switch off the television, put down the cell phone or laptop and stop what you're doing. Concentrate on what your loved one is saying rather than your emotion or response to what's being said. Listen to how they feel and repeat what you believe they were saying about how they've been feeling. Refrain from offering advice or reacting until you are convinced you completely understand what they are trying to tell you.

When speaking, use "I" statements instead of "You" statements.

'I' statements force us to be honest with ourselves about our ideas and emotions. They also improve the likelihood that our voice will be heard while decreasing the likelihood that a conflict will occur. Consider "It upsets me when you do xxx," instead of "Why do you always have to do xxx?" Encourage everyone in your household to communicate as much as possible using "I" statements. Try to avoid "You" statements, since they often result in hurt feelings, increased conflict, and almost never fix the issue.

Empower all members of the family to express their emotions and opinions.

Strong families encourage all family members, no matter how young or old, to express their opinions and emotions. Everyone should be able to express themself appropriately using "I" communications. People feel better about themselves, are more receptive to facing difficulties, and are more ready to enable others to express themselves when they feel heard and appreciated themselves.

Families who are strong spend time together.

It can be difficult for families to find time to spend together in today's hectic world. But all connections need care, including the family as a whole.

Family rituals may provide a defined time to gather and give each other the attention you need. This ritual might be sharing a meal, commemorating a holiday, attending church/synagogue together, or going out somewhere as a group. It is critical that this ritual be consistent and that no other activity disrupts it.

Family rituals help us identify ourselves as a cohesive group. They provide an opportunity for the family to spend time together, share experiences, and reconnect. Knowing that our family will spend time together can help us cope when we are away from them. Even if both parents work, children may know that they will have some "special time" with parents every evening, every weekend (or whenever works best for the family).

Every child is unique and needs some one-on-one time with their parents.

Giving your child "special time" aids in the development of a deep bond with them. If you can make it a habit, your child will be able to rely on it, and will look forward to this time with you. Make certain that this "special time" is not disrupted by other activities. Don't answer calls or allow other distractions to draw you away from time with your child.

Allow your child to have a say in how you spend this time together. Maybe they'll want to read stories, sing, do some art, go to the playground, play a game at home, etc. The more quality time you can spend with your child, the stronger your bond will be.

Look for ways to connect with your children.

According to researchers, one of the most significant things families can do is spend frequent, short periods of time engaged in child-preferred activities (Sasson, 2021). Make up stories while doing chores, discuss their worries on the walk to the grocery store, read a book while dinner is in the oven. We often believe that we must wait for our "special time," but all of these little moments help us remain connected in between more planned periods.

Strong families resolve their disagreements fairly.

Conflict exists in all families; it is a normal element of human interaction. But strong families work through disagreements by concentrating on the issues at hand rather than by tearing one other down.

SETTING GOALS FOR YOUR ROMANTIC RELATIONSHIPS

We all know that one couple who sets the bar for what we think of when it comes to relationship aspirations. Perhaps it's a friend and her spouse, your grandparents or other family, or maybe even a famous couple with seemingly hectic schedules.

There are many things that keep couples together. Oddly enough, compatibility is not necessarily at the top of this list. Plenty of effort goes into developing effective, healthy partnerships, and this is where relationship objectives come into play.

Setting objectives may be a useful tool to help you, as well as your partner, develop as a couple, whether you've found yourself in a recent love situation or want to improve your current longstanding relationship. Having objectives aids in the formation of stronger bonds between partners, as well as in the resolution of conflicts, and in increasing pleasure.

Don't worry if sitting down together to create objectives seems challenging. In this section, we'll look at why love goals are important to establish at any point in a relationship and how to develop relationship objectives as a couple.

If you're looking for a companion, consider your dating objectives. What are the characteristics of optimal, healthy relationships? What intimate relationships do you fantasize about? How would you and your partner stay on the same page or handle a disagreement? How do you like to be loved by a partner? How would you and your significant other interact most effectively?

The first step in establishing and setting relationship objectives for yourself and your potential mate is to have a clear image in your mind of what a good relationship looks like. Whether you're currently in a love scenario or are still dating, take some time to focus on what you need and desire from a potential partner.

A relationship objective is something you wish to do, learn, or experience more with your mate. Regardless of whether a couple's objectives are long-term or short-term, they should be reachable. Setting a lofty goal like winning the lottery or traveling the globe together might be exciting to fantasize about – but if you want to use goal-setting to build and enhance your personal relationship objectives, it's better to establish love goals that are quantifiable and feasible for both of you.

These goals must also be something that both you and your partner are passionate about. Setting one-sided relationship objectives is much less likely to succeed. Goals should be centered on areas of your life where you both have a vested interest in growth and are excited about working on because they'll benefit the future of your relationship.

How to set healthy relationship goals

Here are some pointers for creating relationship objectives with your significant other.

Select a neutral location to discuss relationship objectives.

Whether you live together or apart, find a spot comfortable for both of you to have an intimate but productive discussion. Wherever you choose, it should be a place where you can both be honest and open about your relationship objectives.

Determine the duration of each relationship objective.

Take care that you allow enough time for each goal to be accomplished, but try not to create goals that are so far into the future that you can't see progress. If this is your first time making objectives as a couple, you may want to set some for the next three weeks, three months, a year. Understanding and expressing love via your partner's love language is often an effective method to reach shared objectives. Relationship objectives may take time, but not all of them have to be long-term projects.

Schedule check-ins for each relationship objective.

Just because you've calculated that it will take twelve months to reach a certain love goal doesn't mean you shouldn't work on it on a regular basis. Whether you do it officially on a calendar or simply check in on your objectives every now and then, accomplishing goals needs continual effort from both parties.

Include at least one enjoyable relationship aim.

Your list of objectives should not be all-consuming. Make it a point to include at least one enjoyable goal that you want to accomplish as a couple. For example, setting and keeping to a weekly dinner date, flirting more, or dressing up for each other regularly are all ways to make the process pleasurable. (Sasson, 2021) Including activities and behaviors that you're both enthused about helps it feel more exciting and less like work.

Make certain that your connection objectives are quantifiable.

Let's assume that one of your relationship objectives is to improve your communication skills. How do you assess the achievement of that goal? Less fighting? More closeness? Increased sentiments of love and vulnerability? When setting your relationship objectives, talk about how each one will be assessed and how you both define success. This will make your progress easier to see.

Consider how your love objectives make you feel.

Once you've created your list of objectives, go through it with your partner and discuss how reaching each of these goals would make you feel. Reaching these objectives should leave you feeling happy and satisfied, not anxious or fatigued. This doesn't mean they won't require effort, only that you both see the value in reaching them. If any of them fail the vibe test, scratch them from the list before you proceed.

Make certain that your objectives are equally weighted.

Is there a goal on the list that your companion wants but that you don't agree with or that doesn't connect with your own goals? Ideally, your objectives should be prepared with equal participation and consent from both of you. If an objective is important to one partner but not the other, working toward it as a unified front might be difficult.

DECIDING WHICH RELATIONSHIPS/FRIENDSHIPS ARE TRULY WORTH KEEPING

Friendships may bring out the best in us, but they can also undermine our will to live with dignity, as well as clarity. A friend is essentially a family member whom we have selected for ourselves. They keep our secrets and often see us at our most vulnerable. Quality companions also help us learn about the importance of loyalty and help us demonstrate our inner strength.

While certain friendships might help you develop as a person, others can tear you down and are not worth keeping. Some friendships are little more than the gathering of recreational buddies in an effort to alleviate boredom or because they're convenient. Some friendships are merely fronts to improve one's social image because it feels good to be thought of as someone worthy of hanging out with. Then there are the friendships that can deteriorate into nothing more than self-congratulatory rituals, or a reciprocal scratching of the back. Let's consider which friendships are worth keeping:

The person who does not dismiss or denigrate you

Mutual respect is the cornerstone of long-lasting friendships. Humans are prone to patterns and we all make mistakes. Even the brightest minds of our time invariably made a few poor decisions as they traveled their path in life. A good friend does not enjoy mocking your life or your decisions. Someone who constantly reminds you of your faults or who tries to make you feel like a fool in front of others is not beneficial to your self-esteem. Anyone who attempts to humiliate or attack you, and convince others that you're unworthy is no friend. We are all accountable for the image of ourselves that we present to the world, so if we wish to be trusted by others, we must be aware of those around us who are working against us.

The one who is truthful

If they hang out with us, they may call themselves our friends, but these could be people with ulterior motives, like needing something to do or someone who will listen to them, but who does not reciprocate. We must value more highly the existence of friends who have the desire to help us learn about life, pick up a new skill, overcome a bad habit, hone a craft, and those who introduce us to other interesting people, help us adapt to a new place, figure out an industry, or encourage us to participate in a new life experience.

Such companions aren't simply warm bodies who show up at parties and pose for photographs with you. They are people who value you and want to assist you in improving the quality of your life. Never dismiss the presence of such friends. Their sincerity will give you the confidence to explore other aspects of your personality and live a more fulfilling life.

The one who does not divide or reign over your life

Friendships may become possessive. Such friendships are often founded on immature conceptions of ownership over other people's emotions and time. This is unsustainable and may be oppressive. Friends who strive to have you all to themselves or who force their agendas on you can cause stress and irritation.

Those whose goal seems to be to transform you into a chess piece in their master plan for their own life are likely seeking to separate you from more important people and find ways to control you. If you become a 'yes man' to someone who is attempting to bully and fling you about according to their whims, you're likely to feel lured into circumstances that make you uncomfortable and don't align with your own wishes.

The one who gives you the space you need when you need it

We all benefit now and then from some alone time and seclusion. A good friend will recognize your desire to re-calibrate and collect yourself or spend some time reflecting. Friendships must be realistic and grounded on the awareness that everyone has good and bad days. We all experience adversity and suffering at some point in our lives. A true friend will recognize there are times when you need to be alone and deal with things without the meddling or forced advice of others. A good friend respects your needs and does not try to save you when you do not need saving.

The one who is not a leech

In certain friendships, one person is a taker and the other a giver. This results in an imbalanced relationship. Some friends drain their friends' resources by manufacturing crises simply for the attention it brings them. They demand their friends' emotional, financial, physical, and intellectual resources to be on tap for them, with little regard for reciprocation.

These people don't know when to take a step back. These are the friends who are always in need of money, time, solutions, and attention. A relationship is built on the principle of reciprocity, and if one friend is overreaching or wearing out another, it's important to evaluate if such a connection adds value or just causes exhaustion.

As you consider your friendships, remember that a good relationship may get you through bad times. Nevertheless, as our decisions continue to define us, a friendship is one such decision that may either open or close our eyes, depending on who we let into our lives.

So far, we have covered a great deal that is necessary for constructing a definition of the things we may want in a relationship. But our journey does not end here. In the following chapter, we will focus even more on you as a person and on ways for you to see your worth.

4

KNOW AND LOVE YOURSELF FIRST

The purpose of this first segment is to imbue you with the feeling of being someone important the instant others meet you. When we experience a surge of elation - for example, when we realize we've won something, our eyes brighten and our lips stretch into a broad smile of confidence. This is what winners tend to look like. They move with assurance through the world. They stand tall and have a look of pride on their faces. Good posture indicates that one is accustomed to being on top.

But to help us stand tall, like a *Somebody*, we need a strategy. Flawless posture, perfect equilibrium, and perfect balance are essential for winners.

Let's use a gymnast as an example of how to conduct ourselves as winners. One misstep, one drop of the shoulders, one hesitant movement could spell the end of a gymnast's career. I'll never forget seeing Cirque du Soleil for the first time and watching the elegance and grace of the acrobats as they performed their mind-boggling feats and then rushed to the middle of the big top to take their bows. It is still vivid in my mind. Their heads were high, shoulders back, and they stood so tall they seemed to float above the ground. Every one of them radiated pride, confidence, and the joy of living.

So how can those of us who are not circus performers feel like winners who are used to feeling the sense of pride, achievement, and delight in being alive?

Let's begin with a simple question:

HOW WELL DO YOU KNOW YOURSELF?

Most of us can name our favorite meals, books, movies and television shows. But how deep does our self-awareness go? Are we able to draw links between our past and present or assess how our emotions may be influencing our actions? When life becomes difficult or chaotic, we may experience profound change. We may even detach from ourselves and lose access to our deeper reservoir of knowledge.

Why is understanding oneself so important?

Before we get started with activities to help us become better acquainted with ourselves, we need to understand why knowing ourselves better is as important as knowing which medications we're taking or where to put the gas in our cars.

Here are some of the best reasons:

RESPONDING TO LIFE MORE EFFECTIVELY

Gaining a better awareness of ourselves allows us to be more accountable — or responsible — to life, so that we can respond rather than react. (Heston, 2020) Deeper reflection keeps us from drowning in challenging circumstances and emotions, helping us to make more informed, deliberate judgments. Instead of being overwhelmed by stress, greater self-awareness allows us to recognize when we are stressed and change our path to become more grounded and balanced.

We cannot allow unresolved emotions to influence our behavior.

Many of us, without ever realizing it, harbor anger, sadness, humiliation, and other emotions that manifest in unexpected and perplexing ways. We may strike out at loved ones, causing conflict, we may engage in harmful behaviors or keep company with destructive people. We may avoid challenges out of fear of failure or embarrassment. Discovering and understanding repressed emotions can help us regain control of our life.

Let's create the life we genuinely want.

Knowing ourselves allows us to have a more meaningful and fulfilling life. Understanding our desires and beliefs, as well as taking the time to understand our emotions, helps us to engage in activities that construct an authentic life.

How to Discover More About Yourself

There are several methods to engage in self-discovery, ranging from finding activities that connect with you to actively dissecting deep-seated emotions. Below are a few.

Examine your responses.

Being conscious of your physical self and how it reacts to the environment around you may provide essential insight into your deeper inner existence. Why? Oddly enough, our bodies can tell us a great deal about ourselves without our conscious knowledge.

Instead of responding immediately when you have a powerful physical feeling, stop for a minute and consider the following questions:

- What am I experiencing in my body?
- What sensations do I observe when I focus my attention on my physical self?
- What was stated or done immediately before my reaction?
- What memories from my past come to mind?
- What do I need, and how do I want to be heard?

Start a dream journal.

Our dreams are often mysterious or bizarre - but that's exactly the idea. Consciously granting room and time to that which you may not completely comprehend can be an effective method to gain a deeper awareness of yourself. (Heston, 2020)

Our minds may work through challenging issues while we sleep. Our emotions may surface in the safe haven of our dreams. Below are some suggestions of how to maintain a dream diary:

- Place a notepad and a pen on your bedside table.
- As soon as you wake up, write down what you recall from your dreams.
- Record what occurred, how you thought, what you felt, and any precise information, no matter how insignificant it seems to be.
- Consider any links between your dream and your present or previous sentiments or events, as well as any repetitions or themes that recur over time.

Maintain a regular diary as well.

In general, journaling is a process of sifting through the detritus of the mind, pulling into the light what lies under the surface of our consciousness.

Journaling helps us understand our mind's story and to securely and nonjudgmentally express and process ideas, feelings, and emotions, even the most difficult ones. Journaling may be done in various ways, including utilizing particular prompts, constructing lists, or simply writing down anything that comes to mind at the time. It is entirely up to you to choose the best method.

To start, try the following:

- "I am now experiencing..."
- "I can't stop thinking about..."
- "I really wish I didn't have to..."
- "Today, I'm having trouble with..."
- "When I shut my eyes, the first thing that comes to mind is..."

Think about your ideal day.

Take the time to consider what is important to you – and why. Your perfect day could be something that occurred in the past or something that you hope will happen in the future. (Heston, 2020) Consider your satisfying day from sunrise to bedtime, answering the following questions:

- When I wake up, how do I feel?
- What rituals do I follow?
- What do I notice?
- What am I smelling, tasting, and hearing?
- What do I do with my free time?
- How do I feel throughout the day?
- What do I feel when I reflect on my day before going to bed?
- Why is today a happy day for me?

Find your drains and pick-me-ups.

Make two lists to help you utilize your self-awareness to create genuinely fulfilling days. One list is of activities that energize you and make you feel like the greatest version of yourself. The other list is comprised of things that do not fit with you and that make you feel like the worst version of yourself. For example, is an overabundance of activity and people-pleasing dragging you down? These lists can help you reset. Wait a few days, then pull them out and review them with someone who knows you well to see if any trends emerge.

Embrace meditation.

Try being alone with yourself. Living in the reality of our experiences is what meditation is all about. It is the discipline of being able to be precisely who, where, and how we are in the moment.

While meditation can be a little tricky to get the hang of, doing it on a daily basis (even just for a few minutes) might help you normalize the practice and enjoy its introspective benefits. If you're new to meditation, you may want to start with a guided practice. Meditation apps are an excellent place to begin. They guide you through the first stages of building a practice and help you to make it a habit. Guided meditations for self-compassion include a range of supportive cues to help you concentrate on your meditation.

Make a note of it.

Take out some paintbrushes, markers, or crayons, whether you're an artist or can barely draw a stick figure. Examine your body to see what feelings occur. Then, depending on those sentiments, choose colors and forms. When we concentrate on colors, forms, and sensations rather than on words, we link ourselves to aspects of ourselves that may not yet have a vocabulary but which carry essential clues as to what is going on under the surface.

Concentrate on what makes you feel bad.

While it is not comfortable to investigate negative events or sentiments, doing so may yield a lot of information. When you encounter difficult situations or painful sensations, write down what occurred and what ideas emerge, and then ask yourself:

- What is this moment teaching me?
- What old habits am I repeating?
- Is it fear or shame that drives my actions?

GETTING TO LOVE AND ACCEPT YOURSELF

Accepting the realities of your existence sounds like a simple task, right? But many of us are stuck in our own interpretation of reality, due to any number of things, like remorse, disappointment, ignorance, or merely a hope for something better—a promotion, the kids to grow into successful adults, retirement, and so on. Some of us have clothes in our closet that haven't fit us in years because we haven't connected with the reality of where we are today. (Jacob, 2020)

Giving up the false version of your life and learning to embrace yourself, your present life, and your truth are two of the best things you can do for yourself. Even if the situation you are in is unbearable, remember, the first step is positive: improvement.

Here's how to finally embrace yourself:

Allow yourself to mourn the loss of not achieving (exactly) what you want.

When a child is born, their parents begin to make plans for the future. They imagine what the child will become; they wish for a certain skill/profession, financial status, romantic status, and so on. But when the child becomes an adult, they may choose a different path for their own future.

Even if the change is favorable (maybe they become an engineer instead of a doctor), parents might mourn the loss of their goal for their child. Maybe you've had a similar experience. Maybe you had a dream about what you wanted to do with your life but it was never fulfilled, and even if you succeeded in other ways, maybe you're saddened by the loss of that particular dream. Allow yourself to mourn, and don't feel guilty about doing so. Grieve your loss, let it go, and then move forward.

Forgive yourself.

Learning to forgive ourselves is the foundation upon which we are able to build a happy and meaningful life. I cannot emphasize enough how important self-forgiveness is for creating a happy future. Begin with anything you wish to improve about yourself or your life. (Jacob, 2020) Feeling guilty is like a stone slung around your neck, dragging you down and stopping you from:

- Recognizing how lovely you are (both inside and out).
- Accepting yourself for who you are, flaws and all.
- Hearing and listening to your inner voice of knowledge.
- Feeling sufficient.
- Moving on after learning from your errors.

You've punished yourself enough! Now is the moment to forgive yourself. Maybe you don't even know why you feel guilty; you simply do. Forgive yourself for both real or imagined flaws and errors. Since they both seem equally real to you, treat them equally. Treat yourself with care and empathy, knowing that you have always done your best. Love and accept yourself just as you are, and begin with self-forgiveness.

Be more appreciative of yourself.

Allow yourself the opportunity to become the finest version of yourself. Get there by emphasizing your strengths and demonstrating to the world your abilities, talents, and expertise. If you tear yourself down, nag, and bully yourself for what you can't accomplish or aren't doing, life is not only difficult and stressful, but it also feels long.

Consider the irony of that last remark. Most people grumble about how short life is, but it might seem to many people that life is too long and troubling. Nobody is flawless, and life isn't either, but it could be beautiful and full of pleasure and joyful sensations. Accept yourself as you are, and you will learn to love yourself. Be less self-conscious and tell yourself that for every flaw you have, you compensate with hundreds of wonderful traits.

Increase your self-esteem.

Most things in your adult life begin with you; you are the one who makes yourself feel happy or bad. You have the ability to dismiss negative feelings about yourself. Your thinking creates your self-esteem. Be psychologically tough, recognize your genuine worth, and capitalize on your talents and abilities. Remember that you are the most important person to please in life.

Overcome feelings of inferiority toward others.

Have you noticed that you're much more competent than you believe? Chances are you've done things you never imagined you'd be able to accomplish, whether academically, professionally, artistically or in some other way. Confidence does not rise from the ether; it is built on your triumphs.

It is time to love and accept yourself just as you are and to overcome any feelings of inferiority you have in relation to others.

Explain what it means to you to love and accept yourself just as you are.

- Are you able to admit that you, like the rest of us, aren't perfect?
- Do you agree that you, like the rest of us, have limits and flaws?
- Do you acknowledge that some of the things you want in life are probably out of your reach?
- Do you accept and love other people in your life despite the fact that they're not perfect and may do things that you dislike?

Consider how much compassion you are ready to extend to others but not to yourself. Self-acceptance and self-love shouldn't be influenced by what you can achieve today or the expectations of others. Having a desire to improve yourself does not imply that you are less than. It simply indicates that you realize and cherish your abilities and are prepared to utilize what you currently have to improve and build a more evolved version of yourself. Self-improvement is a step forward, not a step back. Live your life according to your own ideals, values, and beliefs, and you will experience greater self-love and acceptance.

Make an impact.

The first step in making a change in the world is to love and accept yourself as you are. Imagine a society devoid of self-defeating emotions and ideas. (Kos, 2022) A society in which individuals understand the importance of loving and accepting others by first loving and accepting themselves. That sounds like an amazingly healthy and thriving society, doesn't it?

The world does not need another Einstein, Mother Teresa, or Jimi Hendrix; the world requires you just as you are. You are distinct and valuable, and this is what gives you the ability to make a difference. You'll never know what kind of Einstein lurks inside you until you give it a chance to emerge. Plus, it doesn't take another Einstein to have an impact in the world; it takes YOU, affecting one life at a time. Begin by accepting and loving yourself just as you are!

YOUR RELATIONSHIPS SHOULD BENEFIT YOU, NOT HARM YOU

Because social support is such a crucial element of being human, when social interactions fail or are damaged, it can have a harmful effect on our mental health and well-being.

It's also important not to depend on only one relationship for everything you need. Instead, concentrate on building a social support network with a range of various forms of connections — from romance to friendship to work colleagues — to sustain your well-being and overall quality of life. (Kos, 2022)

Any two individuals who support, encourage, and aid one another practically and emotionally likely have a healthy connection. Keep in mind that good communication is the cornerstone of every healthy relationship.

Below are some pointers for building healthy relationships that will benefit you.

People in healthy relationships tend to:

1. Listen to one another and converse without passing judgment. In love relationships, for example, this includes speaking openly about sex and intimacy to ensure both parties are satisfied with their sexual relationship.
2. Respect and trust each other.
3. Make time for each other on a regular basis.
4. Remember specifics from each other's lives.
5. Participate in healthful activities together.
6. Collaborate as a team rather than as individuals.

Most of us have heard the saying, "You always hurt the ones you love." It's easy to let our hair down and display our ugliest side toward the people to whom we are closest, isn't it? But people in good relationships are able to maintain self-control so they don't treat their partner harshly just because they are so close it feels acceptable to do so.

While you don't have to be romantically attached to garner the advantages of a good relationship, there is evidence that a strong romantic connection may improve your health. (Kos, 2022) Here are five advantages of having healthy relationships. Some only apply to romantic relationships, but others apply to any close relationship.

Reduced stress

Being in a steady relationship is associated with lower levels of cortisol, a stress hormone. This shows that those who are in a relationship are less susceptible to mental trauma and that the emotional and social support that comes with having a partner reduces stress. There is even data that shows that cohabiting couples are happier than those who do not live together. Knowing that someone loves and respects you while you go about your day, even if they are not physically there, is a mental health enhancer.

Improved healing

Whether it's having somebody to encourage you to take your medication or having a companion to help take your mind off things, research shows that long-term couples who have had heart surgery are significantly more likely than single patients to survive the first three months following surgery. Long-term partners also described feeling increased safety in their capacity to deal with post-surgical discomfort and less concern about the procedure in general. In other words, a little emotional support may go a long way toward assisting someone in recovery after an operation or illness.

Healthier habits

Good relationships set the tone for a healthy lifestyle in general. If friends, lovers, or other loved ones support healthy eating habits, working out, avoiding smoking, etc., it's more likely to encourage you in that direction. It's much easier to avoid bad habits and engage in good ones when you have someone who supports you in doing so.

A stronger feeling of purpose

Many of us want to feel like we're doing something nice for others and making the world a better place. Being in a close relationship of any kind may provide a person with a feeling of well-being or purpose. The bonus is that having a feeling of purpose can add years to your life!

Increased lifespan

Speaking of adding years to life, research shows that having social bonds might help us live longer. Of course, everyone is different and has different wants and aspirations when it comes to relationships, stress management, and having a meaningful life. If you prefer your own company, that's okay, but attempting to build a few intimate connections might provide obvious advantages to your mental and physical health.

Having at least one very close friend (or trustworthy coworker, family member, therapist, or counselor) to help you manage challenges like depression or anxiety is invaluable, and may also be just what you need. Even one or two solid, healthy connections in your life could improve your health.

THE FIVE PEOPLE IN YOUR LIFE

Most of us have probably heard the famous saying by motivational speaker Jim Rohn: "You are the average of the five people you spend the most time with." In other words, the people we spend the most time with shape who we are.

Consider your environment. Make sure you're spending time with people who share your goals for your life (ideally, people "better" than you, to raise your average). But the truth is, this is only the beginning of the formula. Of course, those around us influence us. But that influence does not end with the five people with whom we spend the most time. Today, it's far more widely distributed, and research implies that it includes people we've never met.

Sociologist and physician Nicholas Christakis and social scientist James Fowler performed the first large study on the scope of social influence. The data they collected provided one of the largest and longest-running health studies ever conducted. People were examined for a number of medical issues, and during interviews, they were quizzed on a variety of survey data, including those concerning family and friends.

The researchers examined the data to discover what the effects of family and friends were on something quite simple and objective: obesity. According to their findings, if a friend becomes fat, you are 45 percent more likely to gain weight in the next two to four years. Interestingly, they discovered that if a friend of a friend becomes fat, your chances of gaining weight rise by around 20 percent - even if you don't know that person! If a friend of a friend of a friend becomes obese, you are still 10 percent more likely to gain weight. There really does seem to be this chain of cause and effect that goes beyond our immediate acquaintances. Our friends cause us to gain weight, but so do their friends, and their friends' friends!

The researchers were able to demonstrate a true chain of consequences between individual friendships (and friends of friends) and body weight gain; they had data spanning three decades. While they investigated a number of possibilities, the concept of norms appeared to be the most likely cause. If a friend is obese, our idea of what constitutes an acceptable body size shifts, and our conduct alters accordingly. Basically, if it's normal for someone else to become overweight, it becomes acceptable for us as well.

The same scenario occurred with smoking rates in a follow-up study. Using the same social network analysis, the researchers discovered that if a friend smoked, the subject was 61 percent more likely to become a smoker. Happiness was perhaps the most telling study. It should come as no surprise that Christakis and Fowler discovered that having happy friends makes you happier. And if a mutual friend of a friend is satisfied with their life, you have a 6 percent better chance of being pleased as well. Six percent may not sound like much, but note that other studies indicate that if I offered you a $10,000 raise, you would only experience a 2 percent increase in happiness!

We think of ourselves as unique individuals, and this isn't a false perception. But the fact remains, human beings are extremely imitative. Our friends really do influence our future. And we don't simply need to be more selective about who we spend our time with; we must examine our entire network and its impact on our life. We need to understand where we fit within the greater network of our social community.

The bottom line: We are the average of all the people around us, not just the five people we spend the most time with. Consider this as you evaluate your surroundings and think about who you are.

LOVE YOURSELF FIRST TO LOVE OTHERS

Is it necessary to love oneself before you can love another? Of course! Loving yourself is the first step toward finding other people who see you for who you are and enjoy your presence. Think of it in reverse: if you don't love yourself, how can you expect other people to love or care about you? Make the decision today to love yourself. When you love yourself for who you are, other people will feel that same loving vibe and energy you emit while you are in their presence. They will want to be a part of that vibe.

Do not misunderstand. When you love and accept yourself, you don't need the affection or approval of others. You are simply more likely to believe that you will meet someone who will love you back. A terrible date or rejection becomes no more than a detour on the path to finding a successful relationship instead of a crushing failure. Because of your self-acceptance and optimistic perspective, you may be quite open in relationships and feel okay with being alone. With this viewpoint, chances are that when you sense a connection, it is real and not motivated by an excessive desire for approval or affection.

If you don't love yourself – if you are judgmental and unsupportive of yourself – you may find it difficult to believe that other people appreciate and love you. When you feel imperfect, you may put space between yourself and others so as to prevent rejection. You might also do whatever it takes to gain acceptance and intimacy, even if it means concealing your true self. But this will only set you up for failed and unfulfilling relationships.

Furthermore, your emotions and fears may impair your judgment of another, causing you to ignore their defects and exaggerate their favorable characteristics. You may find it more difficult to develop a true connection and create a healthy, close relationship as a consequence of your general sense of inadequacy or unworthiness.

So, if there is only one thing you take away from this chapter, let it be this: Loving yourself is the first step to developing amazing relationships in your life.

PART II

COMMUNICATE EFFECTIVELY

5

COMMUNICATION IS EVERYTHING

I realized in my early twenties how important communication skills are for anyone who wishes to live a happy, well-balanced life. I had a few nice acquaintances as a young adult and dated a few men, but I didn't feel particularly connected to anyone. Sure, I could talk to my friends, but I felt there was something lacking. I'd stand around at parties, in class, and in bars, watching people talk and laugh. Small talk appeared to come naturally to them. I assumed I was doing something wrong because communication was not my strong suit.

When I got my first job after college, the same old problems arose. It wasn't that people disliked me; rather, I always felt aloof. I was an introvert who frequently second-guessed myself in conversation and had no idea how to approach people I was interested in.

I felt sorry for myself for a long time. I assumed that some people are just naturally talented communicators, and that practicing social skills if you aren't equipped with a flair for communication would be meaningless. Looking back today, I realize I had a lot to learn. As I discovered, anyone can increase their talents in this area, regardless of age or background.

Our key management tool is conversation. We communicate in order to form relationships with others. By conversing with people, we can influence them. We talk to solve problems, collaborate, and discover new avenues for action. It's wonderful to communicate, yet having a conversation at work can be tricky. A manager recently summarized the issue for me. "This company will not survive unless we re-learn how to talk to one other routinely and on a meaningful level," he told me.

HONING THE ART OF COMMUNICATION: THE 80/20 RULE

When it comes to honing your communication skills, it can often feel like you're lost in a forest of never-ending tactics and techniques, each claiming to be the key to effective communication. But guess what? You don't need to know every technique or strategy in the book. Focusing your energy on a few that deliver maximum impact can do wonders. This is where the 80/20 rule, or the 'Pareto Principle,' comes into play.

The Pareto Principle suggests that 20 percent of your efforts yield 80 percent of the results. So, what if instead of tackling all the communication techniques, we focus on that crucial 20 percent? Imagine the time, stress, and energy you could save while achieving impressive results.

Let's take active listening, for example. It's a small part of communication but a skill that packs a punch. Effective communication isn't just about talking; it's about truly listening to others. Active listening is not merely about hearing the words being said. It's about understanding the sentiment behind them, responding appropriately, and refraining from passing judgment. Perfecting this one skill can significantly enhance the quality of your interactions.

Let's consider a real-life scenario. Employees often complain about feeling unheard or misunderstood in a fast-paced corporate setting. In such a scenario, the 80/20 rule can be used to drive positive changes. If you're a business owner, with just 20 percent of your time and effort devoted to mastering active listening, you can impact how your employees are feeling about being heard or understood.

Just like active listening, several other communication skills can have a significant impact on the quality of your interactions. For instance, when you learn to offer constructive feedback or give a great presentation, these two skills alone can help you establish better relationships with colleagues and clients. So, as you embark on your journey to become a communication expert, remember it's not always about the quantity but the quality of your skills. Master the art of active listening and experience the transformative power of the 80/20 rule in communication.

MODULATING COMMUNICATION: THE KEY TO CONNECTION

Understanding and adapting to the communication preferences of others is not just a skill but an art. It's like being a chameleon, seamlessly blending into different environments while maintaining your unique identity. Adjusting your communication style can make a difference, whether it's for work, personal relationships, or social interactions. Think of yourself as a DJ who can read the room and adjust the music to keep the party going. It's about creating a harmony of voices where everyone feels heard, understood, and valued.

Imagine, for instance, a coworker who appreciates brevity and directness. Now imagine you're involved in a project with them. You habitually add color and humor to your communications, using anecdotes and metaphors, but then notice that they seem distant or frustrated during your discussions. Here's where the power of adaptive communication comes into play, and you adjust your approach to meet their preferences.

On the flip side, consider a conversation with a friend who values depth and connection. Their preferred style might involve lengthy discussions, personal stories, and emotional expressions. A conversation filled with short, crisp statements might leave them feeling dismissed or unappreciated. You can foster stronger and more meaningful connections by being receptive to their needs and modulating your communication style.

Remember, communication is not a one-size-fits-all tool. It's a dynamic ecosystem that requires patience, understanding, and adaptability. It's the difference between a lively, engaging party where everyone is dancing and having a great time versus one where the music is too loud, or the genre is all wrong, and people are anxious to leave. The next time you find yourself in a conversation, remember - it's not just about what you say but how you say it!

LEARNING FROM THE MASTERS: THE CHAMELEON SKILLS OF COMMUNICATION

Have you ever found yourself captivated by a conversation with a highly effective communicator? They seem to possess a unique skill, effortlessly adapting their communication style to suit the situation or person with whom they're engaged. Let's stay with the chameleon metaphor mentioned earlier, because this is an animal with the ability to blend into its surroundings, becoming what it needs to be to thrive. This is not a trait exclusive to a select few people but a skill that can be learned and refined, as we will explore below.

Consider an expert communicator; one minute, they could be breaking down a complex concept to a beginner, using simple language and relatable metaphors. Next, they could be deep in a technical conversation with a professional peer, demonstrating a command of jargon and detailed knowledge. This individual possesses the ability to modulate their communication style in response to their audience's needs.

One of the most notable examples of such an adaptable communicator is the late Steve Jobs, co-founder of Apple. Known for his captivating keynote presentations, Jobs had an uncanny ability to switch from being a visionary storyteller on stage, mesmerizing millions, to being a detail-oriented leader in team meetings, ensuring every aspect of a product was perfect. His standout presentations are still used in business schools worldwide as templates for effective communication, and his team interactions are often cited in management literature as examples of leadership communication.

But this ability to adapt communication styles isn't just a business skill. It's equally valuable, if not moreso, in personal relationships. Think about a time when a friend was going through a tough situation. Did you plow ahead with your usual upbeat, optimistic communication style? Or did you adapt, becoming a quieter listener, offering comfort and support?

So, how does one cultivate this chameleon skill? It begins with active listening, understanding your conversation partner's needs, and adjusting your communication to meet those needs. Whether using simpler language, employing visual aids, or changing the tone of the conversation, every little adjustment has a significant impact.

In the end, it's important to remember that communication is not about delivering a monologue. It's a dynamic interaction that hinges on understanding and responding to the other person's needs. As you continue on your journey to becoming a better communicator, keep an open mind, listen actively, and never hesitate to adjust your style. After all, just like a chameleon changes its colors, a skilled communicator changes their style - effortlessly and effectively.

WHY DO PEOPLE HAVE COMMUNICATION ISSUES?

We all know that no two individuals are alike. Our personalities, feelings, thoughts, ideas, and beliefs are all different from one another. What you consider simple may be challenging for someone else. Some introverts are better off alone; they can't properly deal with or communicate with others because they're too busy communicating with themselves; they can be so focused on themselves that they tend to lose sight of the fact that they're surrounded by other people.

Unless you're an introvert yourself, these people live in a different world than you. This is where the skill of ***listening*** comes into play. It's important to improve our listening skills before we consider how to respond to others. Have you ever had a conversation with someone who is physically present but whose mind seems elsewhere? Isn't it aggravating?

Poor communicators believe that "listening" is simply waiting for their chance to speak while mentally formulating their response. This couldn't be further from the truth. Listening is about giving someone else the opportunity to communicate their thoughts and ideas, to establish an emotional connection, and to demonstrate empathy.

As we continue in this chapter, we'll study the fundamentals of good listening, followed by an exercise that will allow you to put into practice all you've learned. Listening isn't only about allowing someone else to say what's on their mind, although that's valuable. It's also the first step toward personal transformation.

According to Carl Rogers, one of the most influential psychologists of the twentieth century, when someone provides us with the opportunity to talk about ourselves and how we feel, we are able to find the best approach to modifying our beliefs and behaviors. Although seeking counsel from others might be beneficial, we are more likely to make positive changes if we work through our issues on our own, and one of the most effective methods to achieve this is to be able to speak freely to an attentive listener.

Hold your tongue and allow your conversation partner the space they need, even if they ramble or their thoughts don't always seem cohesive. They might want to talk to a few more people before making a decision, or they might need to think about the problem on their own. Try not to become impatient or annoyed! Extend the same courtesy to others that you would like to receive from them.

EMPATHY

In addition to modulating your style to adapt to your audience and practicing active listening, empathizing with others is essential to becoming a first-rate communicator. But what exactly is empathy as it relates to communication? Most of us would probably agree that empathy is what enables us to perceive and comprehend the feelings, desires, intentions, thoughts, and necessities of others. But it is also the capability to support others through actions that allow us to engage with and offer comfort, assistance, or lend an ear to those with whom we empathize. Empathy enlightens us about others' feelings, circumstances, and needs, allowing us to interact with them in a more relevant and impactful way. It involves elevating our Emotional Quotient (EQ), otherwise known as emotional intelligence, to connect and communicate more effectively in our relationships.

I don't think it would be a stretch to suggest that most of us would rather be with an empathetic person who can comprehend, connect with, communicate with, and support us than with an empathetic person who doesn't know how to connect with us. In fact, empathy is currently the subject of intense review and debate, as academics and theorists are revisiting its definition and function.

UNDERSTANDING EMPATHY: THE PRACTICAL PERSPECTIVE

So, let's delve a bit deeper - what is empathy from a practical standpoint? When we're able to put ourselves in another person's shoes to see things from their perspective and feel what they are feeling, we have mastered the skill of empathy. Much like when we read a book and become so engrossed in the emotions and experiences of the characters that we feel their emotions as they feel them, empathy helps us directly connect to another. We have the ability to understand and share the same feelings with another person.

Empathy should not be confused with sympathy, however. While sympathy is feeling compassion, sorrow, or pity for another person's hardships, empathy takes it a step further and allows us to imagine what it would be like to be in their shoes.

Let's consider a few examples of empathy in action. If your friend has been through a recent breakup, you may not feel the same degree of pain that they do, but you can still understand where it comes from and offer comforting words. Likewise, for someone who is happy: instead of envy or jealousy, you feel joy for them. In both cases, you consciously try to understand and share their feelings. Remember, empathy isn't just about understanding; it's about connection. It's about reaching out and saying, "I'm here with you." It's about sharing in the human experience and is part of what makes us social creatures. It's what makes us human.

In some ways, empathy may be described as the social and emotional glue that allows us to form and maintain connections. It's a skill that we all possess in varying degrees — and it's even a trait that many of our animal friends share. Some have it in abundance. While some may struggle to empathize, others are extremely sensitive to the emotions, circumstances, and needs of those around them. These hyper-sensitive people are often referred to as empaths.

The good news is that empathy is a trait that can be worked on and improved throughout our lives. Empathic abilities can be enhanced or suppressed (in extreme cases) at any age. Throughout your life, your empathic ability is fluid and changeable. Think of it as a muscle - something that can be trained, honed, and strengthened with time and practice. It's a skill that underpins emotional intelligence (EQ), a desirable quality that can draw people to you.

It's no surprise that emotional intelligence is not only a sought-after trait in professional settings, but it's also a key ingredient in personal relationships, particularly in romantic ones. Indeed, studies have shown that women are generally more drawn to men who possess high emotional intelligence. Why is EQ such an attractive trait? The answer lies in the evolutionary wiring of our species. We are naturally inclined towards those who can understand and relate to our feelings and emotions, because this signals compatibility and mutual understanding.

Remember, empathy is not an inherent gift; it's a beneficial skill that anyone can develop. If you feel a need to enhance your empathetic abilities, start by practicing active listening during your conversations. Ask yourself: What is this person really feeling? What are they trying to express beyond their words? What might they need from me in this moment? Such reflective questions can help you fine-tune your empathy, gradually making it a natural response during your interactions.

The transformation from empathic practice to an empathic habit is a journey of patience and persistence. It involves continuous self-checks and conscious efforts to empathize. With persistent practice, though, you'll find yourself more attuned to others' emotions, leading to deeper connections, enriched conversations, and ultimately, better relationships in all spheres of your life.

Don't forget about the importance of verbal and non-verbal communication

We utilize verbal communication to educate others, whether about our needs or to pass on expertise. Clarification is an important aspect of oral communication. Many of us have difficulty expressing ourselves properly, which can lead to our actions or words being misinterpreted. Appropriate verbal communication has the power to clear up misunderstandings, and enrich conversations with facts and knowledge.

When strong words are more powerful than action, verbal communication can be utilized to repair a mistake. It can also be used as a tool to persuade, allowing for debate, stimulating thought and creativity, and deepening and forming new relationships. The ability of a creature to communicate successfully is important to its survival, and the richness of its social life is largely dictated by how and what it can convey.

On the other hand, consider how many relationships begin with two people meeting across a crowded room and initiating eye contact. The truth is, 95 percent of communication is non-verbal. A suggestive wink can be more powerful than a well-crafted pickup line. Non-verbal clues such as body language can often communicate more about a person's feelings than they can express verbally. The 7-38-55 rule, developed by Albert Mehrabian, Professor Emeritus of Psychology at University of California, Los Angeles, attempts to measure how much meaning is transferred through verbal and non-verbal communication techniques.

The 7-38-55 rule relates to emotional communication. According to this rule, seven percent of information is transmitted through spoken word, 38 percent through tone of voice, and 55 percent through non-verbal cues.

Many experts have used Mehrabian's insights to describe how humans transmit their feelings. Former FBI chief hostage negotiator, Chris Voss, has extended Mehrabian's findings to the field of negotiation research; he contends that non-verbal cues and body motions transmit significantly more than words during a negotiation. Mastering non-verbal communication, including reading body language, is an essential ability for anyone attempting to enhance their negotiation skills and avoid misinterpretation during formal talks, whether in law enforcement, diplomatic scenarios or the corporate boardroom.

Non-verbal communication has five basic purposes: expressing emotions, communicating interpersonal relationships, supporting verbal engagement, reflecting personality, and performing rituals like welcomes and goodbyes.

In his paper, "The Importance of Effective Communication," Edward G. Wertheim explains how non-verbal communication comes into contact with verbal communication: we can use non-verbal cues like gestures, expressions, and vocal inflection to strengthen, disconfirm, replace, complement, or highlight our verbal communication. When we tell someone we love them, but avoid eye contact, this transmits a different message than saying the same words while looking directly into their eyes, just as a beaming smile when we offer congratulations confirms the sincerity of our words.

ENHANCING NON-VERBAL COMMUNICATION: FOUR PRACTICAL TECHNIQUES

No matter how eloquent your words might be, your body language is consistently communicating far louder. Let's review four practical non-verbal communication techniques that you can begin using today to polish your overall communication skills.

1. The Power of Eye Contact

In an experiment conducted by Yale University, increased eye contact resulted in increased feelings of intimacy. It's simple: maintaining eye contact shows the listener that you're fully engaged in the conversation and consider their words valuable. It's a silent compliment that goes a long way in forming strong connections. Try to steadily hold the gaze of the person with whom you're interacting – you'll find them more captivated by your words and more willing to open up themselves.

2. The Delayed Smile Technique

A smile is a universal language that transcends borders, but the timing of a smile can dramatically change its impact. Next time when you meet someone, don't flash an immediate smile. Instead, pause for a moment, look into their eyes, and then slowly let your smile bloom across your face. This slight delay lends authenticity to your smile and makes the other person feel special and appreciated. You'll be amazed how this tiny shift in behavior can transform relationships.

3. Posture: The Silent Indicator of Success

Posture is a silent barometer of confidence. Studies with monkeys have shown that even our primate cousins associate good posture with social dominance. Try imagining a string pulling you upward through your center and out the top of your head. You'll find yourself sitting or standing taller, emanating an aura of self-assuredness that others will find impressive and be drawn to.

4. The Errol Flynn Technique: Give Undivided Attention

In the age of constant distractions, offering your full attention to someone has become a rare gift. Named after the famous actor Errol Flynn, known for his ability to make anyone feel like the most important person in the room, this technique is about completely squaring your body towards the person you're interacting with. By doing so, you silently speak volumes about your respect for and interest in them. This technique creates an intimate environment of mutual respect and understanding, fostering deeper and more fulfilling relationships.

Mastering non-verbal communication isn't an overnight process, but these techniques provide a solid starting point.

RECOGNIZING COMMUNICATION ISSUES IN YOUR RELATIONSHIPS

Lack of communication can have the following effects on a relationship:

- Conflicts become more serious.
- Your points of view become negative.
- You both turn your backs on one another's efforts to connect.
- One or both of you feels invisible or unnoticed.
- One or both of you experiences loneliness.
- There is a reduction in intimacy.

- Setting and achieving objectives can be difficult.

The following are signs of poor communication in a relationship:
- Criticizing or dismissing one another
- Becoming defensive
- Stonewalling
- Passive-aggressive behavior
- Assuming you have a good understanding of what your companion is thinking
- Arguments recur in a cyclical pattern and are never resolved
- Lack of compromise
- There are fewer efforts to connect with each other
- Arguing on "the facts" of a quarrel rather than focusing on what each person went through

Emotional Intelligence Lessons

Emotional intelligence, as mentioned earlier, is the capacity to recognize and manage your emotions. Sometimes, this type of intelligence makes us unable to organize and achieve goals. An EQ (emotional intelligence factor, or the assessment of emotional intelligence) can range from low to high, and it's rarely linked to cognitive talents like IQ (intelligence quotient).

People who are emotionally savvy may function in both intrapersonal and interpersonal situations. Intrapersonal functioning refers to a person's ability to accurately perceive their own feelings and use that information to navigate their lives. Interpersonal functioning refers to their ability to understand and communicate effectively with others. While these abilities are intertwined in many ways, one may excel in certain areas while struggling in others.

Why You Need to Be Emotionally Stable

Criticisms and rejections are an unavoidable part of life. We can't please everyone, no matter how hard we try, but it can be painful to be on the receiving end of such things. But when you're emotionally stable, you feel more confident in yourself. Despite the discomfort of criticism, you do not let it prevent you from achieving your objectives. You're ready to take the next step.

Having an optimistic mindset is crucial, especially in uncertain times like today. When we find ourselves outside of our "safe" zone, we develop anxiety, mistrust, and worry. These feelings have a tendency to cause us to imagine worst-case scenarios.

Emotional stability allows us to avoid drowning in negative thoughts and instead maintain an optimistic view of the future. Hope that whatever you're going through right now will pass, and believe you'll be able to overcome whatever obstacle you're up against. Loving yourself and understanding yourself is essential to creating amazing, long-lasting relationships with others.

However, for relationships to remain healthy and steady requires communication.

HOW TO FIX COMMON COMMUNICATION ISSUES

I suspect that being interrupted is one of the most vexing experiences for all of us. As we continue, we'll assess how frequently we interrupt others and will begin to concentrate on giving our conversation partners the time and space they deserve. Let's discuss this and other common issues and how to resolve them.

Eyes are remarkable. They teach us things we would never learn through speaking. They can be entrancing, forceful, empathetic, disturbing, perplexing, reproachful, supportive, loving, and so many other things.

The phrase, "One look is worth a thousand words" means that we're able to grasp something in an instant from a look that words cannot convey. Eye contact is undoubtedly the most powerful kind of communication we have, and the power of the eyes is greatest when two people are staring directly at each other - literally gazing into each other's eyes. Your eyes are incredibly powerful communication tools; they can evoke a variety of emotions in those you communicate with. This is why it is so important to maintain eye contact, even after the other person has finished speaking.

Experiments have revealed that children, in particular, respond to basic drawings of eyes in much the same manner they respond to real eyes, implying that they are fascinated by other people's eyes from an early age. They will even respond to circles that resemble eyes because they first make contact through them.

It is possible that such responses are instinctive and linked to basic survival behavior, given that children who make eye contact receive more attention and have a better chance of having their needs met than those who do not. There is little doubt that as we grow older, we learn not to misbehave when an adult is watching us just by paying attention to their expressions.

Because eye contact varies between infants and adults, men and women, introverts and extroverts, and so on, it is critical to consider the context before making readings. Even when people are speaking on the phone and cannot see each other, their eye movements resemble those of face-to-face conversation. In this way, the eyes are the "windows to the soul," and can teach us a lot about the inner workings of our thoughts.

The same is true for facial expressions. The study of facial expressions has long been a subject of scientific investigation. For example, in 1872, Charles Darwin published *The Expression of Emotions in Man and Animals*. Other nineteenth century scientists promoted hypotheses that linked body type, cranial form, and face shape to intelligence, criminality, and even insanity. None have stood the test of time because physical traits are not dependable predictors of behavior or mental condition. A recent study, however, showed that facial expressions can help us grasp what others are feeling and communicating at any given time.

The expressions on people's faces, like eye contact, relay a lot of information about their emotional states. Because the face is often the first aspect of a person that we see, expressions play an important role in shaping attitudes toward us. Pleasure, discontent, intrigue, boredom, fear, and fury can all be read from the way people look at us, and it is these dispositions that regulate and shape how we interact with one another.

We form opinions about others based on what we perceive in their faces. Those with pleasing features are frequently attributed with personality traits that they do not actually possess. In fact, we are more inclined to say that someone with a pretty face is a beautiful person than we are to say this about someone we deem unattractive. Obviously, this is unjust because we are depending on exterior looks rather than substance, but research has shown this to be human nature.

Let's return to my opening remark about interrupting others. If you're in the middle of a heated debate, you might feel compelled to speak your piece as it comes to you. Your enthusiasm or passion for an idea may rise to the surface, discounting all else. But even if our thoughts are brilliant, when we interrupt, our conversation partner likely becomes too annoyed to give them the attention they deserve. By interrupting, we're implying that our views and opinions are more valuable than theirs. Interruptions can derail someone's stream of thought, as you may know from personal experience. They also make people feel insulted.

If someone respects you and your thoughts, they should at least allow you to finish those thoughts, right? When actively listening to others, we must use the same principle. Interrupting can destroy your chances of forming a strong relationship with someone. They will begin to retreat from you if they believe you are more interested in imposing your particular viewpoint on them rather than getting to know them.

Now let's talk about timing. When it comes to talking with your partner, especially about something important, choosing the correct time is important. If something upsets you, tell them, and ask them to sit down and have a conversation, either at that moment or at a scheduled time later. If they are made aware that you wish to speak with them, it can help de-escalate the issue.

Begin with "I" statements and emotions. The way we communicate with our partner can make a significant difference to the outcome. Couples often begin a conversation by pointing the finger and assigning blame to the other. Instead, begin by expressing how you're feeling, not making accusations or lobbing criticisms.

Concentrate on being heard, as well as on listening. Many couples approach talks as if they are contests or disputes to be won. Even if you do not agree with your partner and their opinions, it's crucial to pay attention to the origin of their feelings. They should extend the same courtesy to you. Don't make it a contest to see who can come up with the best idea. Instead, listen to what the other person says and try to understand where they're coming from.

And of course, compromise! Remember that reaching a mutually beneficial agreement is the endgame. The point of discussion (whether about past issues or future plans) is not important here. The satisfaction of finding a compromise is what's key. Regardless of the issue, most issues call for some sort of compromise that will allow both parties to forgive and move on. This can also increase feelings of strength and intimacy between partners.

Remember, it's not only what you say that matters, but how you say it. Others will be more likely to listen to you if you speak at a reasonable volume and pitch. We've all met people who aren't unusually bright or intriguing, yet know how to captivate an audience. These people use their voices to attract the attention of their listeners. Voice development is not limited to actors and singers. Anyone who wants to make a good first impression should understand how to use their tone of voice to their advantage.

Let's take a moment to discuss vocal range, and how to correct some of the most typical speaking errors that we all make from time to time, because it doesn't matter how compelling your message is; if no one is listening, it won't get through.

Reduce the volume of your voice. According to research, people who speak at a low pitch are seen as more capable and independent than those who speak in a breathy voice. Both men and women are affected by this. Whether you like it or not, people assess you based on your speaking voice.

Sitting and standing up straight, remembering to take deep breaths, and counting gradually from one to five as you exhale are all useful methods to help maintain vocal authority. You can also play with pitch by repeating the same phrase or sound (for example, "No") at different pitches and intervals.

Regardless of whether you're interested in developing a good speaking voice, learning how to breathe properly is always going to have a positive effect. You might be wondering, 'Doesn't everyone know how to breathe?' Well, sure they do… but not properly! In fact, most of us breathe through our chests rather than our diaphragms. Yoga and breath-based meditation can help you relax your muscles and promote a steady flow of oxygen throughout your body, which is beneficial to your health.

In the end, boundaries and possibilities of communication are defined by our relationships. We engage in conversation differently depending on who we're communicating with. But conversations can be used to start, fix, or change almost any relationship.

So, as we've learned, a good relationship is built on effective communication, but that doesn't mean it's always easy. Our next chapter is about the power of listening.

6

THE POWER OF LISTENING

"Most people do not listen with the intent to understand; they listen with the intent to reply"
— STEPHEN COVEY, AUTHOR, BUSINESS LEADER AND PUBLIC SPEAKER.

In college, I had a friend I would run to whenever I needed to vent. She would sit through all my rants, patiently listening as I processed my thoughts. She only spoke a few times, asking a question here and there or repeating something I said to help her better understand it. Afterwards, I felt like a fog had cleared, and I had gained clarity. I felt heard and understood. I could sense her genuine care and compassion, and they empowered me to make my decisions.

Looking back, I realize I had experienced the power of listening.

Life has become fast-paced and technology-driven. We are bombarded at every turn by noise and distractions, both literal and figurative. In this chaos, listening has been overshadowed and undervalued. But if we want better relationships with friends, family, coworkers, and even strangers, effective communication skills are essential, and primary among these skills is active listening.

As we discussed earlier, active listening goes beyond simply hearing what others say; we must understand and respond appropriately. To add to the complexity, many things interfere with our listening ability, like distractions, noise, biases, emotions, and assumptions. These factors often prevent us from fully paying attention and understanding what's being said.

Listening requires a conscious effort and an inherent desire to understand another's perspective. Have you ever found yourself in a conversation where you're merely waiting for your turn to speak? That's not listening. It's critical to quieten our internal chatter and fully focus on the person speaking. Attempt to understand the deeper meaning behind their words, their emotions, and whatever it is they're trying to convey.

I often think of the old saying: "We have two ears and one mouth, so we should listen twice as much as we speak." It's a simple yet profound observation that serves to remind us that listening is more than just an act of courtesy. It's a way to connect with others on a deeper level, to understand their experiences, thoughts, and feelings.

Empathetic listening takes time and patience. It's about putting yourself in the other person's shoes and truly understanding their point of view. It's about validating their feelings and acknowledging their thoughts without rushing to judgment or offering advice. At first, this approach may require more time, but in the long run, it saves the time and energy spent on misunderstandings and conflicts.

Before you respond in a conversation, take a moment to organize your thoughts. It's easy to react instantly, especially in a heated conversation. However, pausing to process the information can lead to more meaningful and constructive communication. This little habit can make a significant difference in the quality of your conversations and relationships. Remember, effective communication isn't about speed, it's about clarity and understanding.

TYPES OF LISTENING

Listening is receiving, constructing meaning from, and responding to spoken and/or non-verbal messages. This process involves several steps: receiving, interpreting, evaluating, remembering, and responding. Depending on how closely we follow these steps determines whether our listening is active or passive.

ACTIVE LISTENING

Active listening involves paying attention to what someone else is saying, showing interest and empathy, and responding appropriately. It involves paying attention to the speaker's words, tone, body language, and emotions so you comprehend their meaning and intention and are better able to understand their perspective. Active listening also involves offering feedback, asking questions, and summarizing what we hear to confirm our understanding.

Actively listening means you are fully engaged and interested in what the other person is saying. It involves both verbal and nonverbal cues. For example, nodding your head, asking questions periodically, or paraphrasing something you've heard to ensure you've understood the meaning are all indications of active listening.

Active listening is a conscious effort that demands empathy, effort, attention, and practice. Some key components of active listening include:

1. Focusing - giving your full attention to whomever is speaking, avoiding or limiting distractions, and fighting the impulse to interrupt or jump to conclusions. Focusing can also include making eye contact, nodding, and using verbal cues.

2. Reflecting - includes paraphrasing, or repeating what was said in your own words. This helps to check your understanding of what you heard and shows that you are listening. Use phrases like, "So what you're saying is..." or posit open-ended questions inviting the speaker to elaborate, clarify, or explain their thoughts and feelings.

3. Validating - acknowledging and respecting the other person's feelings, opinions, and experiences in a non-judgmental way.

Positive Outcomes of Active Listening

The biggest positive impact of active listening is that it makes us aware of our listening abilities by bringing attention to how we engage with others in conversations. We become more attuned to our listening habits, strengths, and weaknesses.

Here are some ways active listening can help you gain self-awareness and identify areas of improvement:

1. Triggers self-reflection - As the other person talks, you become more aware of your listening abilities, noticing whether you tend to interrupt, make assumptions, become easily distracted, or mentally drift away.

2. You notice non-verbal cues - As noted earlier, seven percent of information is conveyed through spoken word, 38 percent through voice tone, and 55 percent via non-verbal cues. This means that if you are not picking up on body language, voice tone, or facial expressions, you are missing over 90 percent of the conversation, and are therefore more prone to misinterpreting the information you receive.

3. Active listening helps you comprehend information more accurately and

completely, avoiding misunderstandings and conflicts.
4. Rapport and trust can be built, since you're able to establish a connection with the speaker, making them feel valued and respected. This rapport gives you some influence in their lives because you have shown them you care about their needs and interests.
5. Conflict resolution becomes easier once you understand everyone's point of view, emotions, and concerns. This, in turn, allows you to have constructive dialogue, show empathy and find amicable solutions.
6. You're better equipped to empathize and can offer emotional support on a deeper level.
7. Through active listening, you engage with others and share in their experiences, thus strengthening your relationships with them.

As you can see, active listening is a catalyst for effective communication, empathy, and personal growth.

What Hinders Active Listening?

Active listening can be hindered by several factors, such as:

- A lack of commitment to listen fully to what is being said
- Inability to understand the speaker clearly. This is common when the other person speaks in a language you don't understand.
- Bias against the speaker based on status, mannerisms, appearance, etc.
- Negativity towards the speaker based on your mental, emotional, or psychological perspective of them. For instance, if your ideology differs from theirs, you might express hostility or animosity toward them. This attitude can make us narrow-minded and create barriers to new ideas or thoughts.
- A lack of confidence, which can result in hesitancy to give someone your full attention
- Intolerance or a lack of interest in the message or speaker

HOW TO PRACTICE ACTIVE LISTENING

Active listening is a skill anyone can learn and improve. Here are some techniques to enhance listening skills:

1. **Pay attention to the speaker** - Start by making eye contact and maintain it throughout the conversation. It shows you are attentive and interested in what they are saying.

2. **Remove any distractions** - Create a distraction-free space to have your conversation. This includes removing things like your phone, laptop, or TV and clearing your thoughts so they don't distract you from listening.
3. **Use open body language** - Adopt gestures that convey receptiveness and encourage others to express themselves. Use your facial expressions, gestures, and posture to show interest and attention. For example, smile at them, lean forward, and uncross your arms as you listen.
4. **Avoid interrupting as they talk** - Let the other person finish speaking before offering your opinion or asking questions. It shows you respect them and leads to a more balanced conversation.
5. **Paraphrase and ask clarifying questions** - This will help you better understand what the other person is saying. It also allows the speaker to elaborate and share more. For example, you might say, "So what you're saying is..." or "Just to make sure I understood correctly..." then repeat the main points of their message as you understood them. This helps to avoid confusion or miscommunication.
6. **Give helpful feedback** - Offer encouraging words, support, and appreciation throughout the conversation. Acknowledge the speaker's efforts to communicate, share their thoughts, and express gratitude for their openness.
7. **Reflect on the speaker's emotions and express empathy** - For example, consider saying something like, "You sound frustrated/angry/sad/happy about..." or "I can imagine how you feel..." and then acknowledge their feelings without judging or minimizing them.

By integrating these techniques, you can cultivate active listening habits and improve your ability to fully engage with others. This will nurture your understanding of others, build up your relationships, and facilitate more effective and meaningful communication.

Passive Listening

Have you ever found yourself subconsciously nodding as someone talks, but you're not really paying attention to what they're saying? Or maybe you've interrupted them mid-sentence to make your point? Maybe you've even found yourself rehearsing what you plan to say when someone is finished speaking... while they're still talking. If so, you might be guilty of passive listening.

This is when we hear what someone else says without engaging or showing interest. We are not involved or attentive to what is being said and offer little or no feedback.

One key sign of passive listening is zoning out. Despite being physically present, our mind is elsewhere. Maybe we're gazing into the distance, looking away from the speaker, glancing at our phone, or thinking about something completely unrelated to the topic of conversation. As a result, we miss vital details, fail to grasp the message, and appear disinterested or distracted.

Interrupting is another common manifestation of passive listening. Rather than patiently allowing others to express themselves, we interrupt them with our thoughts or ideas before comprehending what they are saying to us. Cutting someone off or butting in as they talk disrupts the flow of conversation and sends a message that you think your perspective is more important than theirs.

Another telltale sign of passive listening is preparing your reply while they are still speaking. By focusing on formulating your response, you miss important points and are likely to misinterpret intentions, both of which contribute to misunderstandings.

Passive listening is quite prevalent in today's distracted world, and its consequences are far-reaching for both the speaker and the listener. A speaker is likely to feel ignored, frustrated, or disrespected, and a listener is likely to misunderstand, which can lead to conflict or missed opportunities.

EXPANDING OUR EMOTIONAL VOCABULARY: THE POWER OF FEELING WORDS

Think back to a conversation where you felt deeply connected with the person you were speaking to. Chances are that conversation was rich with feeling words—words like "excited," "nervous," "joyful," or "disappointed." These types of words can act like bridges, connecting our inner world to the outer world and allowing others to understand our experiences.

Let's consider a real-life example from a workplace setting. Imagine a project manager who, instead of simply stating that a project is off track, expresses to her team that she's feeling frustrated and worried about the potential impact on their client relationships. By using feeling words, she's not just communicating a problem, she's also conveying her emotional state, which invites empathy and a sense of shared responsibility.

Practicing the use of feeling words in our daily conversations can be transformative. It could mean the difference between saying, "I'm fine" or "I am feeling a bit drained today after that long meeting." While the former closes potential avenues of deeper conversation, the latter opens up opportunities for empathy, connection, and supportive interactions.

The Art of Opening Up: Encouraging Conversation

Often, we find ourselves in situations where a friend, a family member, or a colleague seems withdrawn or unwilling to engage in conversation. It's natural to feel frustrated or helpless in these situations. But my college friend who had the knack for patient listening taught me that when someone is seemingly locked within themselves, sometimes all they need is a safe space to vent, to let out their pent-up feelings. An uncomfortable thought, a nagging worry, a minor annoyance—these bottled-up feelings can often act as barriers to open communication.

My friend would often use an insightful phrase to encourage the process of opening up: "Is there something on your mind you'd like to get off your chest?" This simple, non-invasive question often holds the key to unlocking those emotional barriers. By inviting others to express their thoughts, we're not just making them feel heard, we're also paving the way for open, meaningful conversations. Below are a few more examples of good questions that can really help build a sense of emotional intimacy and connection:

- When's the last time you felt heard?
- If you had to watch one movie 10 times, what would it be?
- What's the biggest lesson you've learned this past month?
- Where do you feel most at peace?
- What's something new you want to do or try together?
- What does your perfect lazy Sunday look like?
- When do you feel most connected?
- What's something you're really interested in right now?
- Have you recently learned anything new about yourself?
- What do you remember loving to do as a kid?

So, the next time you find someone struggling to communicate, remember, sometimes all they need is a little nudge to open the floodgates. Remember, at the heart of every conversation is a human being seeking to be understood and valued.

COUPLES AND LISTENING: BRIDGING THE GAP WITH EMPATHETIC DEEP LISTENING

In relationships, effective communication is the foundation of connection and understanding. However, many people in relationships complain about not feeling heard. This is because of our poor listening skills. Not feeling heard can create barriers and strain the bond between partners, leading to disagreements, resentments, and emotional distance. It can also prevent us from working out conflicts and meeting each other's needs. This is why both partners must recognize their listening shortcomings and work on improving them.

The biggest hindrance to effective listening and communication in relationships is reply-oriented listening. This means that you listen in order to reply rather than to understand. Let's say your partner had a disagreement with their boss, who embarrassed them in front of their colleagues. Rather than fully understanding and empathizing with your partner's feelings, you immediately offer advice and solutions. You tell them not to worry about it or to shake it off as a one-time thing. This (unintentionally) invalidates their feelings and experiences, leaving them feeling unheard and unsupported. Reply-oriented listening is a common pitfall, especially in emotional discussions.

A form of passive listening, reply-oriented listening causes us to fail to hear what our partner is saying, since we are distracted by our own thoughts, feelings, or opinions. We might also interrupt, argue, criticize, or offer unsolicited advice, making our partner feel hurt, invalidated, or become defensive. Other examples of reply-oriented listening include:

- Changing the subject mid-discussion
- Offering solutions or suggestions you think will resolve things
- Making assumptions or judgments, such as assuming your partner's boss also has a bad day, or that your partner was at fault
- Minimizing or dismissing the other person's feelings by suggesting they are making a big deal out of nothing
- Comparing or competing with the other person's situation
- Blaming or shaming the other person
- Rehearsing your response so you fail to pay full attention to your partner

The first step to resolving these issues is acknowledging the listening difficulties present in your relationship. Look for signs of poor listening, such as distractions, interruptions, and a lack of genuine engagement. Both partners may contribute to this challenge, and understanding this can help create a foundation for positive change.

Creating awareness and promoting open dialogue about poor relationship listening is pivotal for growth and improvement. By reflecting on your own listening habits and taking responsibility for your contribution to any breakdowns in communication, you can work together toward building a more attentive and empathetic listening dynamic.

A fundamental part of empathetic listening is practicing understanding-oriented listening. This is a facet of active listening in which the goal is to understand the other person's perspective, emotions, and needs without judging or trying to fix them. Some examples of understanding-oriented listening include:

- Staying focused and present
- Paraphrasing or summarizing what the other person said
- Reflecting or naming the other person's feelings. For instance, "I see this makes you sad or angry"
- Validating or acknowledging the other person's experience
- Asking clarifying or probing questions
- Encouraging or empowering the other person
- Showing empathy, not sympathy

Empathy and sympathy both play a crucial role in understanding the experiences and emotions of others. As we've discussed, empathy involves understanding and sharing the feelings of others, while sympathy is simply feeling sorry for or pitying them without necessarily understanding their emotions. Empathy is the more powerful of the two because it allows us to step into another's shoes and see their perspective, which makes it easier to connect with them.

How to Shift Toward Understanding-Oriented Listening

Listening requires effort, patience, and openness. It also requires respect, compassion, and curiosity. When people in relationships listen to each other in this way, they can bridge any emotional distance between them and create a deeper connection. On top of practicing active listening, here are a few other things you can do to develop empathy and shift toward understanding-oriented listening:

- Cultivate curiosity. Try seeing the other person's perspective, emotions, and needs, and imagine how they feel and what they want.
- Be open-minded and suspend judgment. Don't let your biases, stereotypes, or preconceptions interfere with your listening. Try to understand the reasons behind your partner's behavior or choices.
- Be supportive and respectful. Don't criticize, blame, or dismiss your partner's feelings or opinions. Refrain from changing them or imposing your values on them. Accept them as they are.

Empathy is essential for creating emotional intimacy and trust in relationships. It helps us connect on a deeper level and show others that we care about and respect them. Additionally, we avoid misunderstandings and are better able to resolve conflict more effectively when it arises. Through empathy, we reduce stress and increase intimacy and satisfaction while deepening our bond, and this creates a stronger, more fulfilling relationship. Research shows that couples who actively listen to each other are likely to stay together and grow together, and isn't that what we all hope for?

7

OVERCOMING COMMUNICATION CHALLENGES

As we have learned from the last few chapters, communication is the lifeblood of every interaction we have. It is an indispensable part of personal, social, and professional success, serving as a foundation for understanding, connections, and mutual growth. However, despite its importance, navigating the intricacies of effective communication can elude us.

We struggle to express ourselves or understand others, resulting in misunderstandings, conflict, and hurt feelings. This chapter will explore specific scenarios and communication challenges we might all face at times. We will also learn strategies and solutions to help overcome these challenges and foster stronger connections.

First, let's examine factors that cause or contribute to communication issues.

Cultural differences

People from different cultural backgrounds have varying ways of communicating, such as gestures, tones, idioms, or humor. They may also have varying expectations, values, and norms that influence how they interpret messages. For example, some might value directness and honesty, while others prefer subtlety, especially when dealing with something difficult. If we're oblivious to these differences, we may misunderstand or unintentionally offend one another. Cultural barriers can be overcome by learning about the other person's culture, finding common ground, and respecting and appreciating diversity.

Lack of attention and interest

As we've discussed, effective communication requires being attentive and interested in what the other person is saying. If either of you is distracted or preoccupied, you will not be attentive to the message being spoken or shown through non-verbal gestures. You might also miss important details, interrupt frequently, jump to conclusions, or lose track of the conversation, and this can make the other person feel ignored, disrespected, or unimportant.

Emotional state

Your emotions can also color your judgment and perceptiveness, because they influence how you convey and interpret information. With negative feelings like anger, sadness, anxiety, or stress, you might have trouble remaining attentive, expressing yourself, or empathizing with another, particularly if they are the one who hurt you. You might also be more defensive, aggressive, or sensitive to criticism. On the other hand, positive emotions like happiness, excitement, or gratitude can enhance communication, as you are more open, friendly, and cooperative.

Lack of effective communication skills

Effective communication skills are not innate; they need to be learned and practiced. Sadly, many people are unable to clearly articulate their thoughts, give constructive feedback, use appropriate tone and body language, or ask open-ended questions to better understand what they've heard. But without these skills, we cannot build rapport, trust or understanding with others.

Language barriers

Communicating with someone who speaks a different language or dialect can be hard, especially when they use jargon or terminology we are not familiar with. Language differences also create stereotypes and prejudices based on linguistic differences, which can color one's opinion. However, such barriers can be overcome by learning the other person's language (or some of it) or using a shared language. Using simple and clear words, avoiding slang and idioms, and asking for clarification when needed can help to bridge this gap.

Personality traits

Your personality directly influences your communication style and preferences. For example, introverts are more indirect and passive, so they may prefer written communication over verbal communication. Extroverts enjoy talking and socializing, so they might be more outspoken, direct, and assertive. These personality variations can lead to misunderstandings or conflicts if you don't respect and appreciate each other's strengths and weaknesses.

Information overload

The amount and quality of information exchanged during a conversation matters. Too much can overwhelm or confuse the receiver, while too little leaves people guessing or even assuming the worst. Irrelevant, inaccurate, outdated, missing, or biased information can misrepresent the message or lessen its credibility. Filtering and organizing information before communicating it to others is essential to avoid such pitfalls.

External factors

External factors like noise, distance, time constraints, or technology issues can also hinder communication. They affect our ability to actively listen and respond appropriately, leading to frustration, confusion, or miscommunication.

While there are many things that can affect our ability to communicate effectively, the above factors are the most common, so being aware of them can help you avoid or overcome them.

COMMON COMMUNICATION CHALLENGES IN RELATIONSHIPS

In his book, *A Theory of Human Motivation*, renowned psychologist Abraham Maslow proposed that five core needs form the basis of human behavior. This hierarchy of needs tells us our need for love and belonging is as rudimentary as the need for food, water, and shelter. We meet these needs through human interaction and by forming bonds with family, friends, and coworkers. However, emotional intimacy from sexual and/or romantic relationships is pivotal to achieving a feeling of elevated kinship.

This basically means that we enter into romantic relationships to fulfill our core need to be loved and to belong. Studies have even shown that our brains respond to social pain, such as rejection and pleasure, as intensely as physical pain and pleasure (Eisenberger, 2012; Hsu et al., 2015). In other words, our physical, emotional, and mental well-being depends on positive interpersonal relationships, especially romantic ones. So a breakdown in our relationships due to poor communication can be extremely detrimental.

Let's review a scenario that illustrates some common pitfalls of ineffective communication in a relationship:

Anna and Ben have been dating for a year. One evening, while having dinner, Ben brings up something he has been thinking about.

Ben: "Hey, babe, I was thinking... maybe it's time we moved in together."

Anna (looking up from her plate): "What? Move in together? Are you serious?"

Ben: "Yeah, why not? We've been together for a year, love each other, and spend most of our time at each other's places anyway... it makes sense to me."

Anna (shaking her head): "No, it doesn't make sense to me at all. We're not ready for such a big commitment, plus we have different lifestyles and habits... so living together this early on would be a disaster."

Ben (frowning): "Wow, you don't have to be so negative and pessimistic. Could you at least consider thinking about it?"

Anna: "Consider what? It's a bad idea, and I'm not interested."

Ben (raising his voice): "Well, maybe you're not interested in me either. You sure don't seem to care about our relationship as much as I do. Maybe you're just with me for fun and convenience."

Anna (rolling her eyes): "Oh, please. Don't be ridiculous. You're being unreasonable and unrealistic. You want to rush into things and pressure me into something I don't want."

Ben (crossing his arms and sighing defeatedly): "Fine. Whatever. You obviously don't get it."

Anna (sighing): "Yeah, I don't get it. I don't get you. I apparently don't care. You never listen to me or respect my feelings. You always criticize and blame me for everything whenever I don't agree with you."

Ben (turning away): "Well, you reject and attack me for everything."

Anna (getting up from the table): "I do not. You know what? I'm done with this conversation. I'm done with you."

Ben: "Wait, what?"

Anna (grabbing her coat and purse): "I'm leaving. Don't bother calling me."

Ben (staring at Anna, shocked): "Anna, can we please talk about this?"

Anna (before slamming the door behind her): "No!"

Anna and Ben clearly love each other, but their failure to communicate effectively has escalated a small issue into something worse. They did not practice active listening but instead interrupted, dismissed, judged, accused, and ignored each other, resulting in criticism, contempt, defensiveness, and stonewalling, which are four of the behaviors that John Gottman, renowned psychologist and researcher on relationships, calls the "four horsemen of the apocalypse." They can erode trust, intimacy and satisfaction, leading to conflict and resentment.

Here are the issues we've just seen in the Ben and Anna scenario:

Not actively listening

One of the most common communication challenges in relationships is when one or both partners do not listen attentively to each other. This can lead to misunderstandings, resentment, and frustration, as with Anna and Ben. Ben thinks it's a good idea for them to move in together, but Anna doesn't feel like it's the right time, so she doesn't give Ben's idea any actual thought and immediately dismisses him.

Solution: The solution is to practice active listening. Being attentive to what your partner is saying without interrupting or judging them, and expressing empathy and understanding by reflecting on what they say or asking clarifying questions is a recipe for successful communication. For example, rather than saying, "What? Move in together? Are you serious?", Anna could have asked, "Really? You think it's time we move in together?" and then let Ben explain his reasoning.

Criticism and defensiveness

Another common communication issue is when partners criticize each other and become defensive. They attack the other person's character or personality rather than focusing on the specific behavior or issue that bothers them. This can damage the self-esteem and trust of the partner who is being criticized and create a negative cycle of blame and counterattack. Defensiveness helps us deny responsibility and make excuses for our actions rather than acknowledge our role in the problem or apologize for our mistakes. It often involves counter-attacking or playing the victim.

Solution: The solution is to use constructive feedback, which means expressing your feelings and needs without attacking your partner's personality or character and taking responsibility for your actions and emotions. For example, instead of saying, "You never listen to me or respect my feelings," Anna could have said, "It hurts me when you misinterpret or dismiss my opinion." As for Ben, rather than saying, "Well, you reject and attack me for everything," he could have said, "I'm sorry if I came across as pushy or impatient."

Stonewalling

During an emotional conversation, it's not uncommon for one or both partners to shut down or withdraw. This often involves avoiding eye contact, crossing our arms, turning away, giving the silent treatment, walking away, or breaking up. This reaction can make the other person feel ignored, rejected, or abandoned, preventing any resolution or connection.

Solution: To resolve stonewalling, both partners need to remain engaged and responsive. This means acknowledging your partner's attempts to communicate and expressing your own feelings and needs calmly and respectfully, while seeking help if you feel overwhelmed. For example, instead of completely shutting Ben down, Anna could have said, "I'm feeling overwhelmed and angry right now. I need some time to calm down and think."

Contempt and disrespect

When one or both partners shows contempt or disrespect for each other, it damages how they communicate. This includes mocking, name-calling, eye-rolling, sarcasm, or insults. For instance, when Anna tells Ben not to be ridiculous, unreasonable, and unrealistic. By mocking and insulting his suggestion, she is eroding the love and respect she has for him.

Solution: To resolve feelings of disrespect and contempt, both partners must show appreciation and admiration for each other. This means expressing gratitude, praise, affection, and respect for them and avoiding any words or actions that could hurt or humiliate them. Choose words that are kind, honest, and constructive. Use "I" statements instead of "you" to express your feelings and needs without blaming or insulting your partner.

We tend to want our partners to see things our way, but they are not us, so this is impossible, and this attitude gives rise to these and other communication difficulties. By applying the principles of active listening, clear expression, and emotional management, we can enhance our communication skills and enjoy more satisfying and harmonious relationships.

Lack of Quality Time

With the endless responsibilities and distractions of life, carving out quality time for meaningful connections can be a significant challenge. Many couples get caught up with everyday tasks, leaving little room to nurture their relationships. Not spending enough time together leads to feelings of disconnection, loneliness, and even resentment. However, recognizing and addressing this challenge is the first step toward reclaiming and revitalizing relationships.

Solution: Intentionally make conscious efforts to spend quality time with your partner. Schedule and protect this dedicated time. Whether it's a weekly date night or simply spending time together, treat this time as a non-negotiable priority. Practice mindfulness and show genuine interest in your partner's conversations, thoughts, and feelings. By being present, you create a nurturing environment that fosters deeper connections. Remember, the goal is creating *quality* time, not simply increasing the amount of time you spend together.

Financial Communication

Talking about money can be a sensitive and stressful topic for many couples. Differences in financial goals, spending habits, and money attitudes can create barriers to effective communication. Additionally, the fear of judgment or stirring up conflict due to financial decisions can further complicate money discussions.

Solution: Establish open and transparent communication about finances. Set shared goals and budgets, and discuss spending habits, savings, and investments. Create a safe space to discuss your financial concerns or disagreements without judgment, criticism, or resentment. If needed, seek professional financial advice to help navigate these financial discussions together.

COMMON COMMUNICATION CHALLENGES AT WORK

Communication is a vital skill in any workplace, but it can also cause frustration and conflict because of the different personalities, cultures, expectations, or feedback styles. Communication difficulties affect productivity, performance, and morale and contribute to poor decision-making and unfair treatment.

Poor communication at work also breeds a lack of trust and frequent disagreements. Here's a look at some challenges and how to overcome them:

Lack of Transparency and Clarity

A lack of transparency creates distrust and hinders effective collaboration. When information is withheld or not shared openly, it means some people don't know the whole story. Throw in unclear expectations, vague instructions, and ambiguous messages, and you have the perfect recipe for confusion and incorrect assumptions based on speculation. This can negatively affect productivity, morale, and cause serious errors.

Solution: Strive for clarity by providing specific instructions and expectations. Use clear and concise language, ask for clarification when needed, avoid making assumptions, and encourage open dialogue to ensure everyone is on the same page.

Passive Listening

Passive listening is as prevalent in the workplace as it is in almost any aspect of life. Failing to pay attention and engage with a speaker means we can miss valuable information, which in turn can lead to misunderstandings, miscommunication, and missed opportunities.

Solution: Apply some of the techniques we covered in Chapter Six to enhance your active listening skills, such as being attentive, maintaining eye contact to capture non-verbal cues, and avoiding distractions. Also, show empathy, ask clarifying questions, and summarize or paraphrase what you hear to ensure you understand.

Language and Cultural Barriers

In diverse work environments, language and cultural differences can be roadblocks to effective communication. As mentioned earlier, these barriers can create stereotypes and prejudices based on linguistic differences.

Solution: Be mindful of these barriers and make an effort to bridge the gaps. Use clear and concise language, avoid jargon, and be patient in understanding different cultural norms and communication styles. Foster an inclusive environment where everyone feels comfortable expressing their thoughts and ideas.

Biases

We all have our biases, and they can hinder our ability to effectively communicate. For instance, a miscommunication with a coworker might cause them to misunderstand your intentions or actions. These biases can breed mistrust, undermining collaboration, teamwork, mutual respect and active listening skills.

Solution: Give everyone the benefit of the doubt, and don't let biases lead to false assumptions or stereotyping. Be open-minded, listen to what is being said rather than what you are expecting, and avoid jumping to conclusions.

Information Overload

Staying updated on important information at work is vital. However, having to deal with excessive amounts of data can be incredibly frustrating. Having to wade through endless emails, phone calls, or other messages means there's a chance important information will fall through the cracks. It also interrupts workflow, negatively affecting performance and productivity.

Solution: Information is king at the workplace, but how we receive that information matters more. The goal is efficient information processing. Implement strategies to manage information overloads, such as streamlining communication channels, setting clear expectations for the type and frequency of communication, and utilizing information organization tools or techniques.

Encourage effective time management and prioritize tasks based on their importance and urgency. For instance, opt for instant messaging, or face-to-face or video meetings for urgent discussions. Also, provide guidelines on how to share relevant and concise information to avoid overwhelming team members. Make sure to assess and refine these practices regularly to optimize information flow and reduce overload.

Information Siloing

On this same note, when information is not effectively shared, it leads to communication failure and poor performance. Siloing information is basically poor information sharing. In many workplaces, departments work independently, so they don't share information, which results in inefficiency, duplication, errors, and missed opportunities. Additionally, storing information in varying formats limits how quickly employees can find it, leading to time wastage and frustration.

Solution: Implement cross-functional collaboration initiatives and knowledge-sharing platforms. Encourage transparent communication channels and promote a culture of teamwork and collaboration across departments and teams.

Conflict and Disagreements

Having a difference of opinion is a natural part of workplace dynamics, but if not managed properly, it can break down communication and hinder productivity.

Solution: Foster a culture of open communication and encourage respectful dialogue. Create opportunities for team members to express their perspectives and resolve conflicts through constructive discussions. Implement conflict resolution techniques and consider involving a mediator if needed, to facilitate constructive discussions and find common ground.

Lack of Engagement, Feedback, and Recognition

Having employees feel disengaged because they lack feedback and recognition can decrease motivation, productivity, and overall job satisfaction. We become disinterested and disconnected from work if we lack a sense of involvement and acknowledgment.

Solution: Create a culture of engagement, feedback, and recognition. Start with fostering a positive work environment where everyone feels valued and motivated to collaborate. Offer sincere, constructive criticism that's development oriented. Encourage a culture of peer-to-peer recognition, where staff can appreciate and acknowledge one another's contributions. This creates a supportive and collaborative atmosphere.

Effective communication is critical to a productive and harmonious work environment. Recognizing and addressing the challenges listed above is key to promoting collaboration, reducing misunderstandings, and fostering a positive work culture.

COMMON COMMUNICATION CHALLENGES WITH FRIENDS

Do you ever feel misunderstood by your friends? Or like you've struggled to express yourself clearly in a group chat? Do you have friends who never listen to you, always interrupt you, or talk about themselves non-stop? Do you wonder how to deal with conflict without damaging the friendship? You are not alone.

Our friendships play a vital role in helping develop our sense of belonging. However, because of our differences in personalities, preferences, and perspectives, we may experience communication difficulties. Below are a few of these challenges, followed by practical tips on how to deal with them.

- Not listening actively or attentively to each other. Maybe you are distracted by your phone or inner thoughts while your friend shares something important or personal.
- Not expressing one's feelings or needs clearly or honestly. For instance, being hurt or angry at your friend's behavior but not telling them how you feel. These negative feelings can grow into frustration and resentment.
- Lack of intimacy or closeness occurs when you don't share your thoughts, feelings, and experiences with each other. This can make the friendship feel superficial, distant, or unsatisfying.
- Not respecting boundaries, opinions, or preferences. This can make a friendship feel intrusive, controlling, or disrespectful. For instance, a friend may pressure you to do something you don't want to do or invade your privacy.
- Misunderstanding or misperceiving each other's words or actions. For example, thinking your friends are ignoring you because they haven't replied to your messages, but in reality they are simply busy or are having other issues.
- Not offering constructive feedback or support. Feedback involves providing constructive criticism or praise. Instead, a friend may criticize you harshly or unfairly or dismiss your problems or achievements as trivial or insignificant, or you might do the same to them.
- Not resolving conflicts or disagreements. Sometimes we avoid talking to each other after a fight or resort to name-calling or insults instead of addressing the issue calmly and respectfully.

These communication pitfalls can affect the quality and satisfaction of a friendship, as well as the trust and intimacy that should exist between friends. It is important to recognize and overcome these issues by developing effective communication skills and strategies. Some ways to improve communication with your friends include:

1. Using "I" statements instead of "you" statements to avoid blaming or accusing each other
2. Using open-ended questions to encourage dialogue and understanding.

For instance, if your friend is afraid to speak their mind, questions can help them open up.

3. Listening empathetically rather than judgmentally to show interest and compassion
4. Utilizing assertive communication methods rather than passive or aggressive communication to express your feelings and needs respectfully. If your friend has hurt you or made you angry, engaging with them while emotional will not get your point across. It might even make things worse. Wait until you are calmer to better express how you are feeling.
5. Using positive reinforcement instead of negative criticism to acknowledge and appreciate each other's efforts and achievements
6. Using collaborative problem-solving instead of competitive problem-solving to find mutually acceptable solutions. This will show you respect and value the friendship.
7. Using regular check-ins instead of assumptions or expectations to stay connected and updated with each other. Don't assume your friends know how you feel; take care to express yourself well.

Communication is a skill all of us can learn and improve with practice and feedback. By applying the solutions above to overcome communication challenges with friends, family, and co-workers, you can enhance your relationships and enjoy fulfilling and rewarding connections with everyone in your life.

PART III

OVERCOME OBSTACLES

8

SETTING BOUNDARIES

Boundaries help to promote trust and healthy relationships. You are more likely to feel heard, acknowledged, and loved when your privacy is respected. Boundaries are about meeting your own needs, not those of others. You are the one who counts. Crossing your set boundaries is equivalent to verbal, psychological, or even physical abuse.

Your boundaries are the guidelines for how people should treat you and behave around you, how you want to be addressed, and what you will and will not tolerate, all of which are based on your own needs and desires. These requirements are not selfish, impolite, demanding, or self-centered; they are necessary. It's about recognizing your worth, knowing your priorities, and ensuring that others do, as well. Setting boundaries allows you to make time and space for yourself to thrive and achieve your professional and personal goals.

When you are powerful and your feet are firmly planted on the ground, you can be of service to others. And these qualities come from within. Setting appropriate boundaries is an important element of self-care and respect, and it should serve as the foundation for your relationships. This means being assertiveness without being aggressive. Healthy boundaries can assist you in defining your individuality and building your core. (Natalie, 2021) When you firmly say "No" to a commitment, you're honoring the ones you already have. Setting boundaries is not only about getting what you want, it's about having the freedom to live life on your own terms.

> *"The difference between successful people and really successful people is that really successful people say no to almost everything."*

- WARREN BUFFET

Setting healthy limits allows you to communicate by expressing your feelings and thoughts in a clear and concise manner. Healthy boundaries can help you achieve the following goals in both your private and professional relationships:

- Listen to and see other people's points of view while maintaining your own
- Demonstrate self-respect by standing your ground
- Avoid future conflict
- Establish consequences for anyone who violates your boundaries

Have you ever been afraid to say no when asked to do something? Have you ever given something to someone, whether it was your time, money, or energy, only to feel used or resentful? These are indicators that a boundary must be established.

When you're in a circumstance that requires a boundary, you'll probably know deep down - it's a gut feeling requiring a change of the dynamics of a relationship. While many of us find this uncomfortable and would rather not have these difficult conversations, consider which is worse: to set boundaries or to continue to feel resentful, taken advantage of or infringed upon.

Boundaries aren't barriers between people; rather, they're markers that help us reciprocate love and care in a healthy way — and a way that looks different for everyone. Setting boundaries allows you to stay in a relationship while maintaining a strong connection.

We run the risk of losing ourselves if we don't set boundaries. Here are a few examples of what can happen in lives without boundaries:

- We begin to hate people for having needs.
- We begin to feel "on edge," irritated, and irritable with others, though we refuse to tell them.
- We begin to lose our ability to concentrate, we may forget things, and may stop caring as time goes on.
- We lose sight of what acceptable boundaries are.
- We have no idea how to deal with someone who is offended by our boundaries.
- We constantly feel "run over."
- Because we constantly feel out of control, we begin to move from crisis to crisis.

- We feel a twinge of sadness when we think about our future.
- Life begins to seem pointless.
- When we think about creating limits, we feel guilty or afraid.
- We never learn how to respond to someone who asks for our time, love, energy, or money.
- Those around us become less responsible as a result of our inability to say no.
- After a while, we may start to feel nothing.
- We feel selfish when we ask others to recognize our limits.
- We feel like we are living for someone else rather than for ourselves.

What Is the Best Way to Set Boundaries?

The simplest way to set a limit, as corny as it may sound, is to speak plainly. Let's review my three-step method for setting a boundary, which can be helpful if you feel you need direction for doing so.

The first step is acknowledgment. One of the most effective ways to begin any conversation is with a declaration of recognition. In other words, identify the reality, often known as 'the elephant in the room' or the issue no one wants to talk about. That's right - say it aloud. For example, "I know there's a problem in this relationship because I haven't been giving you all you need…"

Second, offer an explanation. It's imperative to explain how you feel. Many people struggle with this but this is mostly because they haven't done it before. The easiest approach is to express yourself using an "I" statement. (If you're having problems figuring out what you're feeling, reference an emotion wheel.) Here are a couple of examples:

Example 1: "I'm afraid of what will happen if you keep spending money."

Example 2: "When you ask about my sex life, it makes me feel uneasy."

The third step is to offer. When sharing emotions, it's common to toss them to the person with whom you're conversing in the hope that they'll understand what you're trying to say. But the offer is where you define your limits. Try "What I really want to do is...", or "Something I'd really like to do is...", or "I'd really like to...", accompanied by "How does that sound?" or another question eliciting the person's reaction to your proposed solution.

Example 1 - "I need to place a limit on how much information you disclose to me. I don't want to hear about money unless I specifically ask about it, okay?"

Example 2 - "I'm not going to discuss my sex life, and I'd appreciate it if you stopped asking me about it. Is that something you think you can do?"

HOW TO SET BOUNDARIES WITH FAMILY MEMBERS

Be strong, yet kind. Setting limits does not show callousness. In fact, when it comes to setting boundaries with certain family members, doing so with kindness can be more beneficial than doing it with anger or defensiveness, which could cause them to strike out. Kindness, on the other hand, increases the chances of a peaceful exchange.

Maintain a reasonable level of expectation. It's not reasonable to agree to spend Christmas at a family member's house if you know they'll ridicule you the entire time you're there. Setting and maintaining boundaries is the opposite of giving in or acquiescing to demands that you attend family functions or other gatherings where you and the other person are together. (Kos, 2022) Be honest with yourself about how much time you're willing to spend with that troublesome family member and under what circumstances you're willing to see them.

Be prepared to walk away. Many of us forget that when someone is being toxic, we have the option of removing ourselves from the situation. You may feel compelled to defend yourself, but if a difficult family member is skilled at making you look bad or making you feel awful for exploding after they've been poisonous to you for hours, the best thing you can do is leave. Simply get up and walk out. You are not required to provide an explanation or apology.

Be consistent and assertive. Setting boundaries is not a one-off but a continuous process. You must reinforce them by sticking to them and not allowing family members to cross them or manipulate you. If they do, assert yourself and remind them of your limits. You can say "No" or "Stop" firmly or walk away if necessary.

Respect others' boundaries. Setting limits works both ways. Just as you are asking others to respect your boundaries, you must respect theirs, too. This means you can't impose your expectations, opinions, or demands on them. Ask them about their boundaries, listen to them without judging or arguing, and apologize if you have crossed them in the past, then try to avoid doing so again.

SETTING HEALTHY BOUNDARIES WITH COLLEAGUES AND BOSSES

Setting boundaries with friends and family should be addressed differently than setting boundaries with coworkers. The biggest distinction is how well you already know your friends, as well as your level of comfort in discussing any problems you may have. With our friends, it feels so normal to be able to talk about topics like this, or have empathy, because you know one another so well. But we often spend hours at work with people we don't know all that well. This means that if we don't ask, we may not know what works for them. We don't always have the chance to talk about it in a way that feels comfortable to us. However, just because it doesn't come naturally doesn't mean it shouldn't be brought up and discussed as a group.

When searching for a new job, for example, it is important to prepare for the issue by setting expectations. We often forget that we are evaluating the people and the organization to which we're applying as much as they are evaluating us. (Norris, 2021) Ask pertinent questions throughout an interview to gain a better understanding of the work environment.

Determine the best method to frame the discussion. Let's face it: discussing limits with anyone might feel unpleasant at first. It necessitates a level of dexterity and comprehension that may not always come naturally. When setting limits with a colleague, it's crucial to think carefully about how you'll structure the conversation. Find a technique to speak to them without having the entire conversation revolve around boundaries. This relieves some of the stress or anxiety we may experience as a result of having to have the discussion.

For example, if your manager mentions an email or message that you didn't respond to after regular office hours, you could say, "I don't usually check my email in the evening so I can give my family the attention they deserve."

SETTING BOUNDARIES WITH FRIENDS

Friendships are an integral part of our lives. They provide support, companionship, and shared experiences. There are parts of life that would be a lot harder to get through or overcome without friends. Unfortunately, in pursuit of making and keeping friends, lines can become blurred, and we sometimes forgo setting boundaries in exchange for companionship.

Even in the closest friendships, though, it's imperative to establish healthy boundaries to maintain balance and respect. You are not building a wall around yourself but setting the stage for a mutually fruitful relationship built on a framework that fosters understanding, communication, and personal growth.

Here are some other reasons why you should set boundaries with your friends:

- You feel overwhelmed and don't have the bandwidth to accommodate someone else's struggles. After all. we can't pour from an empty cup.
- Your availability changes; for example, maybe you're at a certain life stage wherein other demands are exhausting you, such as kids or work, and you

can't devote the same amount of time or resources to your friends that you once could.

- It's a one-sided relationship.
- You don't feel safe sharing things with your friends because they may not keep them private.
- Their teasing often goes too far. Sometimes friendships reach a point where we lose sight of each other's sensitivities and we inadvertently hurt one another in the name of fun.
- You have different communication styles that affect how you share and receive information. For instance, you might prefer to call someone if what you have to say is urgent, but they would rather text you.

Setting boundaries with friends can be challenging, especially if you're afraid of hurting their feelings, losing their friendship, or being seen as selfish or rude. However, not doing so could land you in a perpetual cycle of disappointment and frustration. Luckily, there is a way to set healthy boundaries with your friends without feeling guilty.

Identify your boundaries. The first step is knowing what your limits are and why they matter. Ask yourself what you value, need, and what you can offer. These are things that support you rather than detract from your well-being. For example, if you value honesty, privacy, or independence, you want your friends to respect these values too.

A good place to start is by learning your relationship patterns. How you form bonds determines what you allow to happen. For instance, if you have codependent patterns, you learn to put your feelings and needs aside for the sake of others, leading you to repeatedly become stuck in one-sided relationships. To figure out your relationship patterns, ask yourself:

- When is it hardest to say no?
- Why can't I stand up for myself or ask for what I need?
- How long have I been doing this?
- Why did I develop this pattern?
- How is this holding me back?
- What am I afraid will happen if I stop this pattern now?

Open dialogue. Before setting a new boundary, let your friends know what it is and how they can respect it. Be transparent and explain what it is that's bothering you and how you want it to change. Then ask them for their thoughts. Approach these conversations with kindness, honesty, and assertiveness.

Use "I" statements to express your feelings and needs without blaming or attacking them. For example, "I feel irritated when you call me late at night. I need to sleep well to function well the next day. Can you please call me before 10 p.m.?" Phrase it in a way that prevents them from becoming defensive. Be polite but firm, and avoid apologizing or justifying yourself.

Enforce your boundaries consistently. Follow through with your boundaries and hold yourself and your friends accountable for them. If they respect them, thank them and acknowledge their efforts. If they cross them, remind them of what you agreed to and follow through with the consequences. For instance, consider limiting contact, ending the conversation, or distancing yourself from the person. Remember that you have the right to say no and to protect yourself from harm.

Nip problematic behavior in the bud ASAP. If you notice a behavior that's causing you problems, immediately address it rather than waiting until things become worse. If you don't like how your friend teases you, let them know. It can be scary, but it's not as bad as dealing with the consequences of falling out because of the behavior.

The key to discussing issues or problems you have with a friend is to do it early and to approach it correctly. Here are a few tips:

- Don't assume what their intentions were. Explain how the behavior made you feel. Don't attack their character.
- Give them a chance to offer their side of the story and listen with an open mind.
- Own your part in the dispute, and apologize if needed.
- Clarify that you still care and that you value their friendship.
- Be willing to accept their apology and move on.

Emphasize the value of your friendship. No matter how delicately you frame it, boundary-setting can still be hurtful, especially when you have been friends for a long time. However, to soften the blow, emphasize how important the friendship is to you and how having this talk will benefit the friendship. If you did not care, you would simply let the friendship die rather than have these difficult conversations.

Avoid situations where your boundary might be crossed. Sometimes no matter how hard we try, our friend might not be willing to respect our boundaries. If you don't want to end the friendship over it, accept that there are situations where your friendship no longer works, and in which you don't have to participate. Let's say you like going on hikes, but your friend doesn't and complains the entire time, which annoys you. Surely there's no point in hiking together anymore, right?

Compromise and offer alternatives. You will have to meet your friend in the middle if you want to make things work, especially if they have a boundary that directly opposes your own. Compromising is a great way to find common ground and grow a stronger bond. For example, if your friend always calls you at odd hours and it interferes with your sleep, ask them to call you earlier or schedule a weekly call where you can talk for hours. This provides an alternative that serves you both.

Consider leaving the friendship. As difficult as it may seem, sometimes it's impossible to alter an existing relationship dynamic without making significant changes. If your boundary is big, your friendship might fail to evolve to accommodate it, and you might lose your friend as a result. As heartbreaking as this can be, it is a necessary step, since the alternative means being stuck in an unhealthy relationship that no longer serves you.

Setting boundaries with friends can be difficult, but it is also necessary and beneficial for both parties. By setting healthy boundaries, you can improve the quality of your friendships, increase your self-esteem and confidence, and enjoy more happiness and peace in your life.

SETTING BOUNDARIES IN YOUR ROMANTIC RELATIONSHIPS

Communicate your feelings and views openly and honestly. It's important to be honest and transparent with your partner about your thoughts and feelings. Of course it's not always easy to sift out your thoughts and feelings in the moment, so if necessary, ask for some time to think. Just don't use this as a stalling strategy to avoid having to talk about the issue. Also, ask your partner how they are feeling instead of assuming you already know. Each of you must be able to put your thoughts and feelings into words so they can be understood by the other to avoid any guesswork.

You are responsible for your decisions. Do not blame your partner for the problem or for your feelings. Instead, both of you should think about your choices and the role they play in the issue.

Without criticizing your partner, express your thoughts diplomatically. In a heated argument, consider saying something like, "I feel wounded and confused right now," rather than, "You upset me because of the way you're speaking to me." The first one is not accusatory, so will likely be better received.

Self-reflect. Before discussing boundaries with your partner, take time to reflect on your needs, values, and personal limits. You need to understand what you are comfortable or uncomfortable with, such as communication, intimacy, or time spent together. Self-reflection allows you to figure out what your soft and hard limits are. Soft limits are the boundaries you're willing to compromise on, while hard limits are those on which you will not compromise.

Negotiation and compromise. Once you know your limits, you can find common ground and negotiate compromises. The boundaries should be mutually agreed upon, and you should both have the opportunity to express your needs and concerns.

Revisit and reassess. As much as you want to hold your ground and maintain your boundaries, as your relationship evolves, it's important to periodically revisit and reassess. Discuss any changes or adjustments that may be necessary due to personal growth, life circumstances, or relationship dynamics. For instance, when you have kids, your lives will change, and boundaries you set earlier will have to be re-evaluated. Take care to check in with each other to make sure any new boundaries serve both partners' needs.

Be respectful and supportive. Be respectful of your partner's boundaries as you expect them to respect yours. Encourage and support each other in maintaining the agreed-upon boundaries. When boundaries are crossed, address the issue calmly and respectfully, seeking resolution and understanding.

Remember, healthy boundaries in romantic relationships are meant to promote emotional well-being and foster a strong and respectful relationship. They make you feel secure, supported, and understood.

WHY IS IT DIFFICULT TO ACCEPT BOUNDARY SETTINGS?

When a boundary impacts you personally, it can be hard to understand and accept. Many of us did not grow up with models of effective communication, and what appeared to be limits were most likely rules imposed by parents or other parental figures. If we were not encouraged as a child to set our own limits, we may not be able to set or keep boundaries as adults, so it's something that must be learned.

When someone you care about sets a boundary that impacts you, a lack of experience or negative association with rules, along with your internal refusal and threat surveillance system, can cause you to feel defensive or threatened. Your brain may reorganize resources to keep you safe, which is helpful if there is an actual threat, but not so much when it isn't the appropriate response. You may feel overwhelmed, scared, angry, or anxious in response to the perceived threat, and then blame the other person for your unpleasant feelings. (Norris, 2021) In such cases, give yourself a time-out to de-stress and then return to the conversation more engaged.

So, the next time somebody sets a limit with you, thank them for sharing and affirm their boundary by following through on it. And if you have a nagging feeling of resentment or a little voice in your head asking you to say no, speak out and discuss it. It can only be beneficial to your relationship.

People constantly cross my boundaries, what should I do?

Remember, no one is perfect. If your boundary is new, others may need to be reminded of it. When enforcing the boundary, be as compassionate and polite as possible as you remind the person of the agreed-upon understanding. You can even use a modified version of the aforementioned three-step methodology. "I understand that this is a recent boundary, but I was offended when you asked me about money after I told you that the subject was uncomfortable for me and I didn't want to discuss it. I hope you can respect my boundary in the future."

If you care enough for yourself, you'll be strong enough to keep your boundaries on track and will not let someone else force you to do something you don't want to do.

9

HOW TO STOP OVERTHINKING

I believe most people eventually embrace change, once they recognize their power and develop a clearer picture of where they want to be and how to achieve it.

Overthinking, in its purest form, is the act of thinking too much, too deeply, or for too long about a matter. It's when you delve into your own mind, trying to solve an imaginary problem or predict an unforeseeable future. It's when your mind, like a hamster on a wheel, keeps spinning in the same spot, but gets you nowhere.

But why does this happen? The answer lies in the grand theater of our mind, where thoughts are the actors and emotions are the audience. Thoughts, without a doubt, have a massive influence over our behavior. They shape our emotions, which in turn color our days and even our physical sensations. They have the power to lift us, to make us feel energized and creative. Conversely, they can be our heaviest chains, dragging us down into a pit of fatigue and despondency. They can even manifest as physical illness.

The concept of self-talk, the ongoing dialogue we maintain with ourselves, is central to our understanding of overthinking. Have you ever realized how your thoughts sound like a narrative? How they voice your worries, rehearse upcoming conversations, or weave stories about situations that haven't even occurred? This internal monologue is a natural part of our cognitive functioning. It's not a sign of mental instability, but a mechanism through which we try to make sense of our world.

At times, however, this self-talk turns sour. We start doubting ourselves, anticipating disaster, and magnifying past disappointments. This negative self-talk then becomes a source of overthinking, causing anxiety and distress, like a film that keeps replaying the same disheartening scenes over and over.

I like to tell people that the mind is like a garden, and thoughts are the seeds we plant. Some seeds grow into beautiful flowers, giving us joy and inspiration. Others, however, sprout into weeds of negativity, choking our mental peace. The key is to recognize these seeds and choose judiciously which ones to nurture.

This understanding of overthinking lays the groundwork for what's to follow. By understanding the roots of overthinking, we can address its effects and find ways to transform our self-talk, enhancing not only our personal wellbeing but also our relationships.

THE ROOTS OF OVERTHINKING

The reason we overthink isn't simple. Like a diamond, which has many faces, each one shining when the sunlight hits it, the reason we overthink has many faces. Some are due to personal issues; others are due to things happening around us.

Personal Reasons

What are these personal reasons? Let's start with money problems. The fear of not having enough money can cause us to overthink. We worry about bills we haven't paid. We worry about our debt. We worry about not knowing what will happen in the future. This keeps our mind busy with endless thoughts.

Another personal reason is bad things that have happened before. Our past experiences, those that were negative, can come back to haunt us. Picture this: You're in a library, with old, dusty books on a shelf. Suddenly, the books crash to the ground, creating a mess. That's what these past experiences do to our mind.

Then, there's the feeling of not being good enough. Sometimes we think we're not capable or smart enough. This makes us question the decisions we make. This leads us to overthink.

Reasons based on things happening around us

Now let's talk about things that happen around us. These can also make us overthink. What people say about us is one of them. When someone says something negative or critical about us, it can make us think... a lot. It's like throwing a small stone into a quiet lake. It creates ripples that spread far and wide.

Next, we have society's expectations. Society expects a lot from us. The fear of being judged, the need to fit in — these things pressure us and this pressure can cause overthinking.

Remember, overthinking is not a forever thing. It's something we learn to do. And just like any habit, it can be changed. The first step to change is to know why we overthink. Once we know the reasons, we can begin making changes.

Dr. Nicole LePera, a famous psychotherapist and counselor, said, "When we become an observer of our thoughts, we can better understand where they stem from. It is only then that we can learn to navigate them." These words are important. They will guide us as we venture further into understanding the impacts of overthinking and how to deal with it.

NEGATIVE SELF-TALK: THE FUEL FOR OVERTHINKING

As we peel back the layers of overthinking, a significant revelation emerges — the pivotal role of negative self-talk. When we stumble upon a rocky road, it's that persistent inner voice that magnifies each pebble into a boulder, each hurdle into a mountain.

Let's shine some light on this internal monologue. When you stub your toe, do you sigh and say, "Clumsy me, always in a rush," or do you chuckle, "Well, that's one way to wake up!"? When a project doesn't yield expected results, do you berate yourself, "I can never get things right," or do you encourage, "I've learned something valuable for the next try"? That's what self-talk is — your internal response to life's ups and downs.

It's when this self-talk turns sour, weaving a narrative of self-doubt and pessimism, that overthinking takes root. *How does this happen?* It's like a snowball rolling down a hill, gathering mass and momentum with each rotation. One negative thought leads to another, and before you know it, your mind is filled with a barrage of self-defeating thoughts.

Let's consider some examples:

- *Nothing and no one can help me.* Picture yourself in a dark forest, lost and alone. This negative self-talk is akin to closing your eyes, refusing any guiding light, and surrendering to the darkness.
- *My partner doesn't love me.* Imagine seeing the world through gray-colored glasses, where every affectionate gesture seems insincere, every loving word appears hollow. That's the impact of this self-deprecating thought.
- *I can't lose weight.* This thought is like a millstone around your neck, weighing you down each time you try to rise. It drowns your motivation, making each attempt at fitness feel like a battle lost before it even begins.

But why should we care about our self-talk? According to Dr. David Burns, author of the bestseller *Feeling Good: The New Mood Therapy,* there's a direct correlation between negative self-talk and our emotional wellbeing. How we talk to ourselves can significantly affect our mood, behavior, and physical health.

UNDERSTANDING THE CONSEQUENCES OF OVERTHINKING

Overthinking has a large, shadowy influence that extends into our overall mental and physical health, sometimes leading our brain down a dangerous path.

How Overthinking Touches Your Mind

Imagine your mind as a beautiful, peaceful garden. Overthinking is like a creeping vine that sneaks into this tranquil space, strangling your peace and causing uncomfortable feelings like stress and anxiety. Dr. Susan Nolen-Hoeksema, professor of psychology at Yale University, once said that too much thinking can trap us in a cycle of negative thoughts. This makes us more likely to feel depressed. It's like being stuck in quicksand: the more you struggle, the deeper you sink.

Still wondering how this happens? It's all about the power of your thoughts. Your mind is a canvas that's easily influenced, and your thoughts are like artists. These artists paint your emotions, which in turn color your mental state. A busy mind filled with negative thoughts can cause a whirlwind of stress and anxiety that washes away any feeling of calmness.

Physical Health Gets Tangled with Overthinking Too

Overthinking doesn't just mess with our mental health. It also reaches into our physical health. Constant worrying, which often stems from overthinking, can start your body's "fight or flight" response. This reaction is helpful when you're in real danger, but when it's set off all the time because of overthinking, it can cause health problems like sleep disorders, digestive issues, and even heart disease. It's like triggering a false alarm in a peaceful neighborhood - it leads to unnecessary chaos and discomfort.

Some studies suggest that chronic overthinking can lead to loss of cognitive abilities, increasing the risk of dementia and Alzheimer's disease. Famous neurologist Dr. Daniel Amen explains in his book *Change Your Brain, Change Your Life,* that "ANTs — Automatic Negative Thoughts, can steal away the joy in your life and can make you feel out of control." These ANTs, born from overthinking, pose a threat to our cognitive health, making our brains prone to diseases.

The Link Between Anxiety and Overthinking

Anxiety and overthinking feed off each other, escalating feelings of distress. Overthinking magnifies our worries, causing anxiety to flare up. And in return, anxiety fuels overthinking, creating a cycle. Clinical psychologist Dr. Alice Boyes, in her book *The Anxiety Toolkit,* suggests that "Overthinking and second-guessing all your decisions can also lead to anxiety." Understanding this close relationship between anxiety and overthinking can help us manage our mental health better.

OVERTHINKING IN RELATIONSHIPS

In the world of relationships, overthinking can be like a thick fog obscuring a beautiful landscape. It distorts our perspective, turning innocent gestures into suspect actions, and heartfelt words into veiled insults. It's like wearing a pair of distorted glasses, where each glance, each interaction is twisted into loops of doubt and apprehension, straining the bonds we share with others.

Let's consider an everyday scenario. Your partner forgets to call you after work. A simple, innocent oversight, right? But what if overthinking decides to join the party? Suddenly, this forgotten call morphs into an ominous sign. Does she not care anymore? Is he losing interest? These unwarranted doubts, the offspring of overthinking, can create cracks even in the strongest relationships.

Now, that's just one side of the coin. Overthinking in friendships, too, can be equally destructive. Imagine you send a joke in your group chat, but unlike other times, no one responds. Most of us would shrug it off, right? But what if your mind starts overthinking? The silence balloons into a sense of rejection. 'They don't find me funny. Maybe they don't like me.' Such overblown interpretations can sour friendships, creating unnecessary rifts.

Much like a weed in a garden, overthinking can choke the life out of relationships. It breeds insecurity and mistrust, the two most potent relationship killers. But how do we weed out this overthinking? How do we clear the fog and restore clarity? To answer this, let's turn back to renowned relationship expert Dr. John Gottman. In his book, *The Seven Principles for Making Marriage Work,* Dr. Gottman highlights the concept of "turning towards" instead of "turning away." In simple terms, it means addressing issues head-on, communicating openly instead of dwelling in the alleys of overthinking. For instance, if your partner's forgotten call incites doubts, talk to them. Express your concerns. You'd be surprised at how quickly this can dissolve the fog of overthinking and bring clarity to the situation.

Similarly, in friendships, open communication plays a significant role. If you feel ignored in your group chat, speak up. It's possible that your friends were busy or missed your message. By communicating, you uproot the aspersions cast by overthinking, nurturing healthier friendships.

In the words of Mark Twain, *"Some of the worst things in my life never even happened."*

These words hold a profound truth. Overthinking creates a world where doubts replace trust, where insecurity overpowers affection. It's crucial that we recognize these phantoms for what they truly are - illusions. By doing so, we rob overthinking of its power, fostering relationships that are not only stronger but also happier.

Remember, overthinking is a squatter in the house of your mind. It's time to take charge, evict this intruder, and reclaim your mental peace. So the next time overthinking knocks at your door, greet it with understanding, combat it with communication, and watch it retreat, leaving behind relationships that are as clear as a cloudless sky.

DEALING WITH OVERTHINKING - EASY WAYS AND METHODS

Changing Your Thoughts with Cognitive Restructuring

Cognitive restructuring is like having a GPS for your thoughts. It helps you navigate away from negative thoughts and toward positive ones. It helps you challenge your negative thoughts and replace them with positive ones. It's like using a brush to wipe away old, peeling paint and replacing it with fresh, vibrant color.

Dr. Martin Seligman, well-known psychologist, educator and author, says that by changing our negative thoughts, we can have a more positive outlook. He compares it to cleaning a dusty mirror. Once you wipe off the dust, which are the negative thoughts, you can see your true reflection, which is reality, much clearer.

Helpful Tricks to Stop Overthinking

We've talked a lot about techniques to help with overthinking, but there are some simple tricks that can also make a big difference. Here are some of them:

- **Stay moving:** When your body is moving, your mind is too. This can help distract you from negative thoughts. Go for a walk or bike ride, dance to your favorite song, or do some yoga.
- **Keep your choices simple:** Having too many options can make you overthink. Try to keep your choices simple. For example, when you're choosing what to wear, limit your options to a few outfits.
- **Be thankful:** Paying attention to the good things in your life can help shift your focus away from negative thoughts. Take a moment each day to think about what you're grateful for.

Remember, overthinking is just a habit, and habits can be changed.

PRACTICAL EXERCISE

Below are a series of exercises that will help you apply the knowledge you've just gained. Each exercise is like a stepping stone, leading you from the foggy terrain of overthinking toward the clear horizon of calm and tranquility. Let's embark on this journey together.

Three Days per Week Meditation - A Lifetime of Satisfaction

Here's a simple body scan meditation exercise for you:

1. *Lie on your back with your legs extended and your arms by your sides. Close your eyes and take a moment to connect with the surface beneath you. Feel its solidity, its grounding presence. Now, take a deep breath and as you exhale, let your body soften, surrendering to the support beneath you.*

2. *Now, let's journey inside. Shift your attention to your belly. Feel the rhythm of your breath, its rise and fall. If you're finding it hard to connect, you can place a hand on your belly. Let this be your anchor, your home base throughout this exercise. Now, embark on your internal journey. Move from your torso to your left leg, then your left foot. Observe each detail - the toes, bottom and top of the foot, and then the entire foot. Be curious. What do you feel? Any tingling, warmth, or coolness? Take note but don't judge.*

3. *Continue this journey, moving through each part of your body, all the way up to your head. Each breath is a step, each sensation an experience. When you've completed the body scan, return your focus to your breathing. Picture it sweeping from your feet to your head, a gentle wave washing over you.*

To conclude, allow yourself to simply be. Be aware of your whole body, of your breath, of this moment. Remember, practice makes perfect. Try this meditation three times a week, and you'll soon start feeling its calming effects.

Talk Positively to Yourself

Another handy tool in your anti-overthinking arsenal is positive self-talk. Think of it as your personal cheerleader, encouraging you and cheering you on. For example, if you find yourself thinking, "I can't do this," stop yourself. Replace that thought with, "This is challenging, but I'm up for it." Make this a habit. Every time a negative thought pops up, acknowledge it, and then replace it with a positive one. It's like swapping the old, worn-out furniture in your mind with new, vibrant pieces.

Also, don't forget the power of a change of scenery. A simple walk or bike ride can do wonders in shifting your perspective. Your environment is a mirror to your mind. A fresh, scintillating environment can bring the same to your thoughts.

Let's remember the wise words of Dr. Wayne Dyer: *"You can't always control what goes on outside. But you can always control what goes on inside."*

You're now equipped to take on overthinking, so let's seize control and embark on this journey toward a calmer, happier mind. Together, we can make it happen!

In this chapter, we have navigated overthinking, its impacts on your mental health, and its potential to disrupt relationships. The strategies we've discussed - mindfulness, cognitive restructuring exercises, and positive self-talk - are your weapons in this battle against overthinking. These are not just theoretical concepts, but practical, tried and tested methods backed by numerous studies and expert recommendations.

Just as you wouldn't expect to run a marathon without training, don't expect these strategies to work overnight. They require patience, consistency, and above all, self-compassion. Remember, it's not about perfection, but progress. Celebrate your small victories, and don't be too hard on yourself for the setbacks—you're human, after all.

In the words of acclaimed psychologist Carl Rogers, *"The curious paradox is that when I accept myself just as I am, then I can change."* This journey of combating overthinking begins with accepting yourself, flaws and all. It's about acknowledging that you are a work in progress, and that's perfectly okay.

With all this knowledge, we can continue our journey toward healthier, more fulfilling relationships, and can tackle our next chapter, which is about coping with troublesome people.

10

DEALING WITH DIFFICULT PEOPLE

We all encounter difficult people in our lives; it's inevitable. Whether they are coworkers, friends, family, or even partners, dealing with difficult people can cause stress, frustration, anger, and resentment. When dealing with a problematic person, your first instinct might be to tolerate it. However, this will ultimately affect your mental health, since you are the one bearing the negative effects of these interactions.

So how do you deal with someone who is determined to get on your last nerve? The first step is figuring out what makes them difficult.

There is no universal definition of what makes a person difficult. While you might consider someone to be difficult, others may not. That said, there are certain characteristics and personality traits that can be ascribed to difficult people.

A difficult person is someone who exhibits behaviors that are selfish, disrespectful, rude, unreasonable, irrational, or lacking in empathy. (Kristenson, 2022) These behaviors interfere with your goals, values, or expectations and violate your boundaries, rights, or feelings. Difficult people have different motives or agendas and may not be aware of the impact of their behavior, or they may not even care about it.

Reasons for difficult behavior

There are a number of reasons people are difficult:

- Their personality - Some people have personality traits that make them more prone to conflict, such as being aggressive, narcissistic, passive-aggressive, or manipulative. These traits are more apparent when they argue and want to have their way.

- Emotions - Some people have difficulty regulating emotions like anger, fear, anxiety, or sadness. As such, they tend to lash out at others or act impulsively when overwhelmed or threatened.

- Stress - Excessive stress from work or family obligations can trigger difficult behavior. Some cope by blaming others, avoiding responsibility, or seeking attention.

- Unresolved conflict - An unresolved issue that hasn't been dealt with breeds tension, which can trigger difficult behavior, irritability, and frustration.

- Poor communication - Poor communication skills or different communication styles can lead to misunderstandings. This causes difficulty listening and problems expressing themselves clearly or giving feedback.

- Different values - Some people have different values or beliefs from the ones we're used to. They may have different opinions, preferences, or goals than us. They may also have different cultural backgrounds or norms that influence their behavior.

- Triggering events - People who have experienced trauma or some form of abuse may lash out, especially when they feel that same type of behavior is being directed at them.

- Unmet needs - Some people have unmet needs that drive their behavior. They may need recognition, respect, support, or validation. They may also feel that others have unrealistic expectations or demands of them.

Common traits of difficult people

Although difficult people can vary in their behavior and personality, they often share some common traits that make them challenging to deal with. Some of these traits are:

- Resistance - Difficult people tend to resist change, feedback, or compromise. They may be stubborn, rigid, or defensive. They may also deny or minimize their problems or faults.

- Tendency to blame - Problematic people tend to blame others for their issues or mistakes. They may be critical, judgmental, or accusatory. They may also avoid accountability or apologize, but insincerely.

- Need for control - Difficult people tend to control others or situations. They may be domineering, demanding, or manipulative. They may also use threats, intimidation, or guilt to get their way.
- Competitiveness – Many problematic people view everything as a competition they must win. They often try to outdo their peers and stand out, which undermines collaboration or teamwork.
- Negativity - Difficult people tend to focus on the negative aspects of things. They may be pessimistic, cynical, or sarcastic. They may also complain frequently or exaggerate their problems.
- Dramatic nature - Difficult people tend to create drama or conflict around them. They may be emotional, volatile, or unpredictable. They may also seek attention or sympathy from others.

Learning how to get along with difficult people is an important part of life's journey, and can help transform social interactions and connections. It involves learning how to manage your emotions, disappointment, and conflict. If we're unable to navigate relationships with problematic people, we may find ourselves in a world of anger, hostility, anxiety, and a "me vs. them" mentality, which is exhausting and lonely.

Let's delve into how we can deal with difficult people in various facets of life.

DEALING WITH DIFFICULT COWORKERS

On average, we spend about a third of our lives working. So if you have to deal with a rude, lazy, or hostile colleague for even half that time, it will negatively affect your performance, productivity, and even your mental health. Working with difficult coworkers can be challenging, but it doesn't have to ruin your life. Below are a few ways to deal with them.

Stay calm, don't react

Have you ever received a message at work that had you seeing red? Or maybe you were berated by your supervisor for something that was not your fault. One moment they ask you to do something, yet in another they reprimand you for failing to do something else.

Most of us likely have instances where interactions with difficult people at work have triggered a slew of negative emotions. But when a situation is emotionally charged, allowing these emotions to control our actions will only make things worse. (Markway, 2015) We could become defensive and turn into a difficult person ourselves!

When dealing with a problematic person, we must remain calm. A momentary pause can help enable you to find the patience to remain calm and rationally assess the situation. This will prevent you from doing or saying something rash that might worsen the situation, and will help you to react appropriately.

Sometimes difficult people act out merely to rile us up. If we allow them to succeed, it will encourage them to repeat this behavior. Try to ignore disruptive behavior and continue with whatever you are doing.

Staying calm doesn't only apply to the workplace, but to every facet of life. Whether you are dealing with difficult friends, family members, or partners, having a handle on your emotions will give you an upper hand.

Identify the problem

Try to understand the nature and source of the difficulty. Is it a personality clash? A communication issue? A value difference? A performance problem? Or is it personal? This will help you figure out your next steps.

Choose your battles

Decide whether or not the issue you are confronting is worth addressing. Is interacting with this person affecting your work quality or productivity? Is it harming your professional image or career? Is it violating your rights or boundaries? If no to all of these, you can ignore it and simply avoid interacting with this person; however, if it does affect any of these areas, choose your battle wisely. Not every issue requires immediate confrontation or escalation. Gauge the significance of the issue and its potential impact on your work or well-being. Some issues are minor and can be overlooked or resolved without direct confrontation.

Next, prioritize issues by identifying key concerns that could directly affect your job performance or create a hostile work environment. Then focus your energy on addressing them rather than dealing with every minor disagreement or annoyance.

Finally, consider the long-term consequences of engaging in a battle with a difficult coworker, especially if they are in a higher position than you. Will it strain your working relationship further or create a hostile environment? Is it worth jeopardizing your well-being or work productivity? Weigh the long-term effects before deciding whether to address the issue or let it go.

Remember, picking your battles doesn't mean avoiding all conflicts or allowing difficult behavior to persist. It means assessing the situation and deciding whether or not to invest your energy in addressing it.

Communicate assertively

If you opt to confront the issue, communicate assertively and respectfully with the difficult coworker. Use "I" statements to express your feelings and needs without blaming or attacking them, and provide specific examples of the issue and facts to support your point of view. Listen actively and empathetically to their perspective and try to find common ground.

Document incidents

If the difficult behavior becomes persistent or escalates to a point where it negatively affects your work, it's very important to document specific incidents. If a coworker regularly tries to frustrate you, keep a record of the details of their behavior. This documentation can be valuable if you need to address the issue formally with your supervisor or HR department.

Seek conflict resolution

When you do decide to address an issue, approach it with a constructive mindset. Choose an appropriate time and place for a private conversation with the troublesome coworker. Clearly communicate your concerns, focusing on the impact of their behavior on work or team dynamics. Express your desire for a positive resolution and be open to finding common ground or compromise.

When in doubt, seek support or advice from a trusted colleague, supervisor, or HR rep. They can provide an objective perspective and help you maintain your professionalism while determining the best course of action.

Practice self-care

Dealing with difficult coworkers is mentally and emotionally draining. To counter these effects, take care of yourself by practicing self-care activities outside of work, such as exercise, hobbies, or spending time with loved ones. This will help you maintain a healthy mindset and ensure you are better able to handle challenging situations.

DEALING WITH DIFFICULT FRIENDS

Difficult friends can negatively affect your social life and well-being while damaging your trust and loyalty. These types of friends can constantly bring you down, manipulate you, take advantage of you, or betray you. So how do you deal with them without losing yourself or causing more drama?

Recognize the signs of difficulty

Difficult friends may criticize you, blame you when things go wrong, lie to you about trivial things, or gossip about you to others in your circle. These behaviors might be the result of envy of your success, happiness, or relationships. Such people might also be demanding, controlling, needy, disrespectful, abusive, or violent. They always take from you and never give back, trampling over your boundaries, feelings, and needs.

Manage your emotions

Before you talk to your friend, try to identify what is bothering you and what you want from the situation. For example, are you angry, hurt, or betrayed? Do you want an apology, an explanation, or a change of behavior? Once you have figured this out, express yourself respectfully but assertively.

Be empathetic

As you discuss the issue, listen to their perspective and empathize so you can understand where they are coming from and what they are feeling. They might genuinely not know they are being difficult, especially if they are going through a hard time or are having a personal issue that could be the cause of their behavior. Offer them your support and compassion and listen to them non-judgmentally, showing that you care and respect their point of view. Sometimes you might need to help them find resources or solutions to cope with something and encourage them to seek professional help if needed.

Seek a compromise or a solution

After you have both shared your feelings and needs, try to find a way to resolve the conflict or meet each other's needs. You may have to agree to disagree on some issues, but you can also look for common ground or mutual benefits.

Distance yourself from them

Sometimes the only way to deal with difficult friends is to cut them out of your life. If someone clearly shows they don't care for you, and are only looking out for themselves, don't feel guilty if you leave the relationship. You don't owe them an explanation or apology; protect yourself and your mental health. For example, you might say, "I've thought a lot about this, and have realized that this friendship is not healthy for me. I'm afraid I can't be friends with you anymore."

Surround yourself with positive people

We all deserve to have friends who love us, respect us, support us, and inspire us. We deserve friends who make us feel good about ourselves and our life. We deserve friends who share our values, interests, and goals. Seek out people with these qualities and cultivate meaningful and fulfilling friendships with them.

DEALING WITH DIFFICULT FAMILY MEMBERS

Accept the facts

At some point, we all must accept that we can't change difficult family members' personalities or behavior. Recognize that's who they are, and that you have no control over them. Focus your energy instead on what you can control: your emotions and actions.

By focusing on your own feelings and needs rather than on the other person's behavior, you reduce the power they have over you. Acknowledge how you feel and why you feel that way. Then ask yourself what you need and how you can meet those needs without depending on the other person's approval or cooperation. This will give you more internal control and reduce your stress and worry over things you have no control over.

Don't take things too personally

Sometimes when a family member is being difficult, you might consider it a personal attack on you. You might feel they don't like you, and that's why they are behaving a certain way. But as we discussed earlier, sometimes people are difficult for reasons we are not privy to, and unfortunately, we are simply an outlet for their frustration.

By understanding their behavior is not about you, you can avoid taking it personally and reacting emotionally. Remember that we all have our own perspectives and experiences that shape our actions and reactions. What might seem rude or hurtful to you might not be the other person's intent. They might be acting out of fear, anger, habit, insecurity, or stress, and are unaware of how their behavior affects you or others.

Not taking things personally can reduce your stress and frustration and improve your relationships with difficult people. It will also free you from feeling responsible for their happiness or unhappiness and help you focus on your own well-being.

Don't let them be toxic

Just because you choose not to take things personally doesn't mean you should allow the troublesome behavior to become toxic. If the difficult person becomes passive-aggressive, hurtful and intentionally tries to agitate you, it's time to put a stop to their behavior. Set healthy boundaries and make sure they know that this behavior is unacceptable. If they respond positively, work on finding ways to rebuild the relationship. However, should things go south, maintain your cool but remain firm. Do not let them ignore or disrespect your boundaries. Create a buffer zone by seeing them less or, if things become unmanageable, cut them off completely.

Compromise

Compromising with your difficult family member where possible can help resolve the tension. Try to find a middle ground or a win-win solution that meets both your needs and interests. Try to empathize with them and see things from their perspective. Be flexible and willing to negotiate and avoid power struggles or arguments that lead nowhere.

Get help

If the issue is serious or remains unresolved after trying everything we've reviewed here, the next best thing to do is seek support from other family members, friends, or professionals. Before taking any drastic measures, such as cutting them off completely, your support people can provide guidance or intervention to resolve the conflict.

DEALING WITH DIFFICULT PARTNERS

Express your love

When you have a difficult partner, take care to regularly express your love and appreciation for them in ways they appreciate. Show them you care about and value them. Compliment them and give them gifts or offer other gestures of affection. Spend quality time with them and share your interests and hobbies.

Be kind

The expression, "Kill them with kindness" is an effective tactic for dealing with difficult partners. No one appreciates being berated or disrespected; with difficult people, doing this can worsen their problematic behavior. So even though you disagree with their behavior, be kind. Avoid name-calling, insults, or sarcasm. Try to understand their perspective and feelings. Listen to them without interrupting or judging. Ask questions to clarify what they are saying and to validate their emotions, and show empathy. Treat your partner with respect and courtesy, and often this will help resolve difficult behavior.

Resolve conflicts constructively by sticking to the facts

Emotions can run high, and this can make remaining objective quite challenging; however, try to focus on the issue at hand, not on the person. It's possible you might not make them see things your way, so simply explain and avoid justifying yourself or being defensive. If you always fight about the same things, don't bring them up. Consider having a neutral party mediate the situation so you can both keep your emotions in check.

Set limits and stick to them

You've probably noticed that we've talked about setting limits quite a lot in this book. If you are dealing with a difficult partner who is abusive, disrespectful, or dishonest, remember you have the right to say no and even walk away. If you set your boundaries and make them clear to your partner but they ignore them, put your foot down. Don't let them manipulate or guilt-trip you into allowing yourself to be subjected to disrespectful or abusive behavior.

OVERCOMING THE EFFECTS OF DEALING WITH DIFFICULT PEOPLE

As we all know, there are problematic people in every facet of life. While many of these tips will help you deal with them, the most significant thing you can do is fortify yourself so you can withstand and overcome the negative effects of dealing with such people. Let's review a few ways you can change your mindset.

Realize there will always be difficult people

Most of us are aware that regardless of where we live or work, we will likely encounter troublesome people at some point in our lives. The key is learning to identify and handle them, since it's impossible to entirely avoid them. For example, hostile people are prone to reacting violently, even to trivial matters. They are cynical and argumentative, and insist on always being right. When dealing with a hostile person, it's best to avoid them or not engage them.

Increase your stress tolerance

It's important to become more resilient to stress and frustration, as this benefits your health and well-being. Remember, you can't control what someone else does or says, but you can control how you react and whether or not you engage with them. By increasing your resilience, you challenge the irrational beliefs that could trigger stress, anger, and outbursts. When dealing with a difficult person, you might become angry and think, *I can't deal with this*. But you can. It will take a lot of willpower, but it's possible. Your power lies in how you deal with it: will you let it stress you or will you remain calm and assess the situation rationally?

Engage in self-examination

It will come as a surprise to no one that our behavior dictates how others view us. If people continuously attack you, it could be because you attract the wrong personality. If you are overly negative, other pessimistic and neurotic people might flock to you. Take time to assess your behavior and demeanor toward others. Are you aware of your emotions and how they affect you? What about your behaviors and how they affect others? Are you doing something that's contributing to the problem? Or maybe the way you're handling an issue is making things worse.

This self-awareness will help you determine your strengths and weaknesses so you will be better equipped to handle troublesome people.

Be aware of your perceptions of others

Finally, make an effort to become aware of your preconceptions of others. Your friend or partner might seem difficult, but they could be going through a tough time. Rather than immediately judging their behavior, take a step back and imagine things from their point of view. Remember to be empathetic, accepting, and non-judgmental.

PART IV

BE REMARKABLE

11

DEVELOPING FRIENDSHIPS

We all know that friendships are important for our well-being and happiness. They fulfill our need to belong and experience companionship. They enrich our lives, boost our self-esteem and confidence and give us a sense of purpose. Our friendships can impact our physical health, financial fortitude, and even our lifespan. Research shows a direct correlation between the intensity and quality of our friendships and our life satisfaction. (Amati et al., 2018)

So why are friendships sometimes difficult to develop or maintain? Why is it a challenge to find others who share our interests, values and goals?

In May 2023, Google searches for "how to make friends" reached an all-time high, even surpassing searches for "how to make money." This suggests that people today are very interested in friendships and community. Ironically, in an age where we have access to instant connections, our ability to make genuine friendships has deteriorated, resulting in increased loneliness.

The truth is, too many people think friendship is only about hanging out, having fun, and sharing interests. But as most of us eventually learn, true friendship is defined by mutual unconditional love that breeds loyalty, trust, support, and honesty. It involves a different kind of love than we receive from family or a partner. True friendships are the only relationships we enter for the sake of the relationship, not because there's something in it for us. (Big Think, 2023) This type of friendship is about being there for each other through good and bad as we grow and learn.

THE FRIENDSHIP RECESSION

In an age where we seem to have unlimited access to other people, it can seem like making connections is easier. However, this isn't the case. Despite being able to reach almost anyone at the touch of a button (or click of a mouse), the number of close friendships has been declining, and loneliness is increasing.

A survey by the Survey Center on American Life shows more people are spending time by themselves and have less time to devote to their friendships. This, in turn, has led to a stark decrease over time in the number of close friends we have. The survey found the number of people with at least six close friends decreased from 55 percent to 27 percent, and the number of people identifying as having no friends rose from 3 percent to 15 percent.

Several factors have spurred this 'recession':

- **Decrease in time spent with friends** - Life today is fast-paced. Our hectic schedules, long working hours, and multiple commitments leave limited time for socializing and nurturing friendships. Work demands, family responsibilities, and personal obligations also contribute to a decline in the quantity and quality of time spent with friends.
- **Lack of face-to-face interaction** - With the rise of technology and digital communication, there has been a shift toward virtual interactions, which can lack the depth and intimacy of face-to-face interactions. Texting, social media messaging, and video calls, while convenient, may not fully capture the nuances and connection that come from in-person meetings.
- **New responsibilities** - As we transition into different stages in life, we take on new responsibilities, like starting a career, better managing our finances, and building a family. These added responsibilities can consume time and energy, leaving little room for socializing and maintaining friendships.
- **Workism** - The modern work culture, often characterized by long hours, high levels of competition, and the blurring of work-life boundaries, can leave you exhausted and with little time for socializing. Focusing more on career advancement and professional success often overshadows our ability to nurture and invest in friendships.
- **Breakdown of romantic relationships** – When we break up with a significant other, we often lose the friendship groups we forged as a couple.
- **Geographical mobility** - As we relocate for education, career opportunities, or personal reasons, we disrupt existing friendships and make it challenging to establish and maintain long-lasting connections.

The most significant outcome of this recession is the increased loneliness so many of us feel. With the ever-increasing number of surface-level acquaintances and fewer true friendships, we experience an increased lack of social support and greater isolation, both of which negatively impact our physical and mental health. This increases the risk of depression, anxiety, cognitive decline and even cardiovascular disease.

WHY IS HAVING HIGH QUALITY FRIENDS SO IMPORTANT?

It's good for your health

Friendships improve our health on every level. These social connections are just as important as having a healthy diet and working out. Physically, these relationships lower the risk of developing high blood pressure and diabetes in all age groups. (Yang et al., 2016)

Quality friends can motivate you to adopt healthy habits, like exercising, eating well, and quitting bad habits, like smoking. They can also join you in these activities, making them more enjoyable and rewarding. And having friends who support your health and wellness can make you more likely to stick to your goals and overcome obstacles.

They make you happier

Quality friendships bring joy, laughter, and happiness. The Harvard Study of Adult Development found that relationships are the number 1 indicator of joy and happiness. (Harvard Second Generation Grant and Glueck Study, n.d.) The 80-year, ongoing study found that the only factor that directly correlates with our level of happiness is the quality of our relationships.

They provide emotional support

Quality friendships are a source of comfort and support whenever we are stressed, sad, lonely, or experiencing grief. Friends can listen to your problems, offer advice, share their experiences, or just be there for you when you need a shoulder to cry on. They also help you cope with challenges, such as moving to a new place, starting a new job, or coping with a breakup. Having friends who care about you and understand you can make you feel less alone, more confident, and more hopeful.

Social engagement and personal growth

Quality friends expand your social circle and provide opportunities for social engagement. They can introduce you to new experiences, perspectives, and interests, all of which foster personal growth and self-discovery. They can also celebrate your achievements, complement your strengths, and encourage your goals. Having friends who appreciate you and value you can make you feel more confident and positive. They can also offer guidance, share knowledge, and challenge you to step outside your comfort zone.

Networking and career benefits

Friends are valuable information channels and can play a crucial role in your professional life. They can help you access opportunities and provide career advice and job referrals. Building a strong network of friends can open doors to new connections, mentorships, and even potential career advancement.

THE DIFFERENCE BETWEEN TRUE FRIENDS AND FAKE FRIENDS

Making new friends in the modern age can be tough, and it's easy to mistake surface-level acquaintances with friends. But a quality friend does the following:

Accepts you for who you are. A good friend does not judge, criticize, or try to change you. They accept your flaws, quirks, and preferences. They celebrate your strengths, talents, and achievements. They love you unconditionally and appreciate you for being yourself.

Values your time. A true friend respects your schedule, priorities, and commitments. They understand life changes and don't take you for granted or expect you to be available at their beck and call. They make time for you when they can and understand when you can't.

Is kind and compassionate. Real friends care about your feelings, needs, and well-being. They are empathetic, supportive, listen attentively, and offer helpful advice when asked. They will comfort you when you are down, cheer you up when you are sad, and celebrate when you are happy.

Respects your boundaries. A quality friend doesn't pressure, manipulate, or coerce you into doing things you don't want to do. They are respectful of your opinions, choices, and values. They won't impose their views or expectations on you and will be careful not to overstep their role.

Supports you during hard times. A good friend is there for you when you need them the most. They won't abandon, ignore, or judge you when you are going through a trying time. They might not be able to help but will stand by your side, offer their help, and lend a shoulder to lean on.

Is fun to be around. Real friends can make you laugh, smile, and enjoy life more. They share your interests, hobbies, passions, have a good sense of humor, and a positive attitude. They might be adventurous and spontaneous, but even if they're not, they are usually willing to try new things and explore new places with you.

Is honest and trustworthy. A genuine friend tells you the truth, even when it is hard or uncomfortable. They won't deceive or betray you. They are loyal, faithful and keep their promises and honor their commitments.

Encourages you to grow and improve. A real friend wants the best for you and will help you achieve your goals. They won't try to discourage, sabotage or hold you back. They will challenge you to step out of your comfort zone and expand your horizons. They will hold you accountable to your goals and dreams while motivating you to learn new skills and acquire new knowledge, and will inspire you to be a better person.

A fake friend, on the other hand, is someone who pretends to be your friend but who doesn't genuinely care about or prioritize your well-being and happiness. They may use you for their own benefit, manipulate you, lie to you, or betray you. Unfortunately, in this day and age, there are plenty of fake friends to go around, but they can be hard to spot. Let's review some signs of a fake friend:

Self-centered. Fake friends tend to focus primarily on their own needs, desires, and interests. They may constantly seek attention, validation, or material gain from the friendship, without considering your needs or feelings. They have a way of making every situation about them.

Untrustworthy. These friends may spread rumors, lies, share your secrets with others, or talk negatively about you when you're not around. They may also agree with others who insult you or mock you. Some even steal from you, flirt with your partner, take credit for your work, or sabotage your plans. They won't hesitate to switch sides when it suits them and abandon you when things get tough.

Manipulative. Fake friends are only nice to you when they need something from you. They may ask you for favors, money, or help, but they never reciprocate or appreciate your efforts.

Inconsistent and unreliable. Fake friends are inconsistent in their actions, commitments, and availability. They may frequently cancel plans, make promises they don't keep, or fail to follow through on their commitments. They may disappear when you need them most. This lack of reliability makes it difficult to trust or depend on them.

Lacks empathy and emotional support. Since they don't truly care for you, fake friends lack empathy and cannot offer sincere emotional support. They won't listen attentively or provide comfort during difficult times. Their reactions to your struggles may be dismissive, unsympathetic, or lack genuine concern.

Jealous or unnecessarily competitive. These types of friends may become jealous or unnecessarily competitive rather than celebrate your successes. They see themselves as superior to you and feel threatened by your achievements, so they will try to undermine or diminish them. They seek to outdo you rather than support your accomplishments.

Inauthentic and insincere. Fake friends pretend to be someone they are not. They may be overly agreeable, excessively flattering, or insincere in their interactions so you will like them. However, their words and actions won't align, and there will always be a sense of artificiality in the friendship.

Don't respect your boundaries or opinions. Fake friends may pressure you to do things you don't want to do or make you feel guilty for saying no. They ignore or downplay your feelings, preferences, or beliefs and will try to change them to suit their own agenda.

Fake friends can be toxic and harmful to your mental and emotional health. They can lower your self-esteem, motivation and make you feel unhappy, lonely and frustrated. If you suspect you have a fake friend in your life, consider whether they exhibit any of the above behaviors. If so, it is time to cut them off and surround yourself with genuine and supportive people who value and respect you.

Now I'd like to share a few words of wisdom. In life, friends fall into two categories: anchors or sails. Anchors weigh us down and keep us from moving, while sails help us make forward progress. True friends push you to be better, while fake friends prefer to keep you from achieving your goals or dreams. As you consider what kind of friends you have, think about this metaphor and determine if they are anchors or sails.

WHERE TO MEET NEW PEOPLE AND MAKE FRIENDS

Making new friends as an adult is challenging, as many of us know, but it is possible. Here are some tips to help you make new friends from scratch:

Pursue your interests - Engaging in activities and hobbies that genuinely interest you might lead you to meet people who could become lifelong friends. You could also enroll in classes or workshops related to your interests or areas you would like to explore. A shared learning experience can foster fulfilling friendships.

Attend social events - Go to parties, festivals, fairs, local meetups in your community, etc. These events are designed to bring together people with similar interests, so they are often the perfect places to meet new friends.

Join groups or clubs - Consider joining clubs, organizations, or groups that align with your hobbies or interests. For instance, if you are into fitness, consider joining a gym. If you like to read, join a local book club. If your favorite hobby is crocheting, you can likely find a crocheting group in your neighborhood. These are all natural environments for meeting new people and fostering potential friendships.

Volunteer - Nothing brings people together or is more fulfilling than giving back. And it doesn't hurt that you could make friends along the way. Consider volunteering for causes you care about, and as you make a positive impact in others' lives, you could form friendships with like-minded people who share your values.

Utilize online platforms - Explore online platforms, such as social media groups, forums, or apps, that focus on connecting people or local communities with similar interests. A great place to start is dating apps. Most have a "meet new friends" option that could help kickstart your friend search and expand your social circle.

Be open and approachable - All this effort to make friends will go to waste if you are not receptive and approachable to strangers. Smile and maintain open body language, like eye contact, so others will find it easier to initiate conversations with you.

Take initiative - Don't be afraid to take the first step and initiate contact. Introduce yourself, ask questions, and show genuine interest in getting to know others.

Be consistent and patient - Building new friendships takes time and intentional effort, so be consistent, follow up with those you meet, and nurture relationships that show potential. Patience is a vital building block in any meaningful friendship, so don't rush things. Genuine friendships develop gradually over time.

Remember, making friends as an adult requires stepping out of your comfort zone, being proactive, and investing time and effort into building connections. It's okay to experience some setbacks or rejections along the way, but don't give up. With persistence, you'll find people who resonate with you and with whom you can form meaningful friendships.

HOW TO GROW AND BUILD A HEALTHY FRIENDSHIP

Lifelong friendships are precious and should not be taken for granted. As those of you who enjoy them are aware, they don't bloom out of nowhere. They are like woodworking projects that require attention and care as you carve them out and continuously work on them. Lasting relationships of any kind require effort and commitment, something too many friendships lack, which is why they fall by the wayside as life evolves. If you couple this with the gradual decline of traditional institutions like family and marriage, it's not surprising that we see a decline in friendships and an increase in loneliness.

As such, building social connections outside these constructs has become even more important, and that's where friendships come in. Building genuine friendships, though, becomes harder as we grow older. When we're young, it seems like all we have to do is strike up a conversation with someone and we hit it off. But as we mature, our lives change and making new friends isn't always as easy as it used to be. Below I'd like to share a few secrets that can help build friendships that last a lifetime.

Self-acceptance

Admitting you want to make a friend is an excellent first step in the process. As adults, we often feel a sense of embarrassment when we say we'd like to make a friend. This self-consciousness can prevent us from creating genuine connections. By ignoring this feeling, accepting yourself and acknowledging your desire for true friendship, you will take a proactive step toward building meaningful connections.

Being yourself

Authenticity is important when forging new friends. Be genuine and true to yourself, as people are more likely to be drawn to your authenticity than to a persona you've put on. Don't pretend to be someone you're not or hide your true feelings and opinions. A relationship based on false pretenses is bound to fail. A real friend will accept you for who you are and appreciate your genuineness. So if you're goofy, be goofy; if you're bookish, don't hide it; if you're spontaneous or adventurous, don't hesitate to make it known – maybe your potential friend has more in common with you than you think!

Supporting each other

A great friendship is also based on mutual support. You must be there for your friend when they need you, and vice versa. Support means offering help, advice, encouragement, comfort, or simply a listening ear when they are going through a hard time. It also means celebrating their achievements, successes, and joys when they are happy. Support doesn't mean solving their problems for them or agreeing with everything they say or do. It means being empathetic, compassionate, and respectful of their choices and feelings.

Being open, trusting, and trustworthy

These are qualities that contribute to the longevity of any friendship. Openness means you are willing to share your thoughts, feelings, and experiences honestly. It involves being vulnerable and allowing your friend to see the real you. This helps foster a deeper connection and understanding between friends, creating a space where you can both feel comfortable being yourselves.

Trust, for its part, is the foundation of any strong friendship. To call someone a true friend, you must have confidence in their reliability, integrity, and loyalty. This is built over time through consistent actions and behaviors that display honesty, dependability, and discretion. This trust goes both ways, of course; while looking for a trustworthy friend, you must be trustworthy yourself, in order to create a sense of security and mutual respect within the friendship. It will ensure you have each other's backs and reinforces the belief that you can rely on each other. This fosters deeper connections, enhances communication, and creates a strong sense of emotional support and understanding, all of which contribute to the longevity and resilience of a friendship.

Demanding less

Just as your life will change over time, so will your friendship. At some point, neither of you will have as much time and energy to devote to the relationship as you did when you first met. You might think you need to do more, but sometimes all you need to do is demand less. This doesn't mean you should lower your standards but simply be more accommodating with your expectations.

Demanding less is a great way to reevaluate your perspective on friendship rules and what matters in your mutual happiness. If you have a problem within the friendship, it might not be the relationship itself but your perspective of it. For instance, maybe you believe that good friends should spend a lot of time together, and if you fail to do so, you might consider the friendship a failure. But your perception is what has caused the issue, since the friendship is probably just fine even though you spend less time together than you used to. By demanding less and valuing the time you do spend with each other, you will maintain a strong relationship.

Being realistic and willing to forgive

When searching for a close friend, we may take things for granted and have unrealistic expectations. It's important to recognize that your friend is only human and is not perfect. You both have flaws that will cause disagreements and misunderstandings as you grow. Approaching friendship with realism and a practical mindset will enable you to conquer your disputes and reap the joys of friendship.

Equally important is being willing to forgive. To err is human, and no friendship can thrive without forgiveness. Holding on to grudges and resentments can poison a relationship over time. Be willing to forgive your friend for their mistakes or shortcomings, just as you would hope for their forgiveness in return. This will allow you both to let go of negativity and move forward, strengthening the bond between you.

There has to be reciprocity

True friendships are not transactional. You are not looking to gain anything from the relationship other than the bonds of friendship. Reciprocity is a vital aspect of building a lasting friendship. This mutual give-and-take dynamic allows both of you to contribute to and benefit from your relationship. Reciprocity fosters mutual support, allowing you to be there for each other during both good and bad times. It demands that both parties put in a shared effort, investing time, energy, and resources in the relationship.

Reciprocity means there's a fair distribution of responsibilities, activities, and decision-making. It shows you respect each other's opinions and ensures you have a voice in important matters, and this sense of equality further deepens the emotional connection.

Appreciating what you have

Sometimes in our search for closer friendship, we overlook old friends. These are people we were once close to but with whom we've lost touch, or perhaps they're simply acquaintances from our past that never had a chance to evolve into strong friendships. Giving these relationships a second chance can be quite rewarding. Since you are not starting from scratch, you have a better chance of quickly rekindling your friendship.

Showing you care

To create durable friendships, we need to show that we genuinely care for our friend. Not through grand gestures, but through little things that show how we feel. Be supportive even when you don't agree, build each other up, and find ways to express your love and appreciation. Don't assume your friend knows how you feel; even if they do, I think we can all agree it's always nice to be reminded.

Collaborating, not competing

As we discussed earlier, an obvious sign that your friend isn't a true friend is when they exhibit an unhealthy competitiveness with you over everything. They can't stand to see you achieve anything and must outshine you. As you search for a true friend and improve your ability to be one yourself, learn to collaborate rather than compete with potential friends. You both stand to achieve a lot more by working together.

Acknowledging the need for change and growth

If your friendship began early in your lives, understand that as you age, there will be transitions, and how you navigate them will determine if the friendship will last. It must endure through events like marriage, parenthood, geographic moves, breakups, career paths, and a host of other dramas. You won't be frozen in time, and neither will they. Learn to accept the changes in each other's lives and make room for growth.

Communicating effectively

As I've reiterated many times throughout this book, communication is the key to any successful relationship, including friendships. We need to be able to express our thoughts, feelings, needs, and desires to our friend and listen to theirs as well. Be empathetic, non-judgmental and avoid making assumptions about them or their decisions. They can't tell what you're thinking or feeling unless you tell them. Be clear, direct, and respectful, and avoid blaming, criticizing, or judging. Employ pointers from earlier chapters to help you become an effective listener and communicator.

Respecting boundaries

By now, we all clearly understand how important boundaries are. Just as you expect your friends to respect your boundaries, you must respect theirs. Respecting boundaries means asking for permission before crossing them, accepting "no" as an answer, and not taking things personally if your friend needs some space or time alone.

Connecting on more than what attracted you to each other

To remain friends over time, it's important to find connections beyond your initial reasons for forging a friendship. For instance, if you became friends because you work together, the friendship might fade if one of you changes jobs or even departments. If you became friends in school, you might lose touch once you've graduated. A longstanding friendship is one that transcends its origins. Figure out what else you have in common, and you can grow beyond what first brought you together.

Valuing your similarities rather than your differences

In a world where political, religious and moral views are increasingly wide-ranging and divisive, it's critical to approach these differences with mutual respect and keep your shared history and feelings in the foreground. This will help you both remember that holding onto and strengthening the relationship is what's important, not your differences.

Committing to the friendship

One more not-so-secret secret to developing a fulfilling and long-lasting friendship is to spend quality time together doing things you both enjoy. You could take a class together, go on trips, have weekly get-togethers to catch up, and so on. However you manifest it, make time for each other and show that you value having each other in your lives. If there is geographical distance between you, you might have to work a bit harder to maintain the relationship, but if it's a quality friendship, it's worth it. Call, text, have video chats, make plans to visit each other, and do whatever you can to commit to preserving your ties. I guarantee it will make a difference in both of your lives and will fortify your friendship.

WHEN IS IT TIME TO CUT OFF AN OLD FRIENDSHIP FOR GOOD?

As important as friendships are, they can also become toxic, draining, or unhealthy. When you have been friends with someone for a very long time, the lines can become blurred, and you can't tell when it's time to let go. So how do you know when it's time to cut off an old friendship?

As you probably suspect, the truth is there is no definitive answer to this question because every friendship is unique and complex. However, here are some signs that can indicate that a friendship is no longer serving you well:

- You feel worse after spending time with them. If you feel anxious, depressed, or exhausted after being with them, it may be a sign that they are not good for your mental health.
- You have nothing in common anymore. While people change over time, if you find that you have nothing to talk about or enjoy with them anymore, it may be time to let go of the friendship.
- You realize that you don't trust them or respect them.
- You think about it and discover that you are always giving, and they are always taking. If you feel that you are always the one who initiates contact, listens to their problems, or helps them out, and they never reciprocate, it could be a sign that they are taking advantage of you.
- You have tried to communicate and resolve issues, but nothing has changed. If you have noticed problems in your friendship and have tried to talk to them about it, but they have ignored you, dismissed you, or refused to change their behavior, it could be a sign that they don't care about your feelings or the friendship.

If you recognize some or all of these signs, you might want to consider ending the relationship. This is not an easy decision to make, nor a pleasant one to execute. However, sometimes it is necessary for your own well-being and happiness. We all deserve to have friends who love us, respect us, and support us.

12

UNLEASHING YOUR CHARISMA

Charisma is defined as an attractive quality some people have that enables them to captivate and influence others. It is the ability to charm, inspire, and persuade others through affability and presence. Charismatic people have a magnetic aura, unshakeable air of confidence, and an innate ability to connect with everyone on an emotional level using both verbal and non-verbal skills.

Charisma is a quality that perfectly balances warmth and competence. (Van Edwards, 2022) Charismatic people are able to signal information in a symbolic, emotional and value-based manner because they possess excellent communication and interpersonal skills. This power to attract attention and influence others is embodied in how one speaks, what one says and how one communicates.

Characteristics of Charismatic People

Our brains are geared to make judgments when we first meet people, and these judgments inform how we interact with them. (Winston et al., 2002) When we meet someone for the first time, our brain instinctively asks two questions.

- Can I trust you?
- Can I rely on you?

Charismatic people are alluring because they know how to answer these questions and garner our trust quickly. But instant likeability doesn't come easily for everyone. That's why learning how to be charismatic is so vital to being an effective communicator.

Before we learn how to boost our charisma levels, let's discuss what makes charismatic people so alluring. Professor of Organizational Behavior, John Antonakis, from the University of Lausanne in Switzerland, has dedicated his professional life to understanding charisma, and in his decade-long study, he found that while we may not all have instant likeability, we can all boost our charisma with the help of a few tricks. We will delve further into this a bit later, but first, let's review some characteristics of a charismatic personality.

1. They are empathetic.

Connecting and forming relationships with others comes easily for charismatic people because they are empathetic, which significantly improves their emotional intelligence. By empathizing with others, they can see things from someone else's perspective and genuinely feel what they are experiencing. As mentioned in Chapter 5, humans tend to feel an instinctual attraction toward those who have high levels of emotional intelligence.

2. They are humble.

We enjoy being around people who are humble and not arrogant - those who don't show off, name drop or blow their own horn. Despite their achievements, they don't behave as if they are better than others. There is nothing wrong with having high self-esteem and confidence; what separates confidence from arrogance, however, is humility—something charismatic people have in large quantities.

3. They are not afraid to show they are vulnerable.

Vulnerability means putting yourself at risk of embarrassment or judgment. Humans are naturally averse to showing vulnerability, as it's often deemed a sign of weakness, though this is not true. Charismatic people can draw others in because they are not afraid to show vulnerability. We are attracted to them because we can relate to their vulnerability.

Take, for example, renowned author and speaker, Brené Brown. Known for her work on vulnerability, courage, and empathy, Brown has shown that embracing vulnerability can lead to deeper connections and enriched relationships. Throughout her career, she has consistently been open and non-defensive about her own struggles and insecurities, creating an environment where others feel safe and compelled to do the same.

Every time Brené shares her personal anecdotes or tales of vulnerability, people are naturally drawn to her. The raw authenticity she brings to the table fosters a sense of reliability, making others feel comfortable enough to open up to her, almost as if they've known her for ages. This openness and non-judgmental approach reverberates in the relationships she forms, resulting in genuine connections.

Practice being a bit more vulnerable than you are used to. Try a little bit at a time and soon you'll realize that your sense of connection and relationships with others has improved.

4. They have a sense of humor.

Humans love to laugh. We are wired for humor. Laughing releases physical and emotional tension, elevates mood, enhances cognitive functioning, and increases friendliness. (Mora-Ripoll, 2010) The benefits laughter has on the human brain are what makes having a sense of humor such a vital skill for charismatic people.

5. They are present.

In an age where distractions are everywhere, charismatic people know the importance of being mindful and present in the moment. This skill allows them to hear and understand what someone else is saying, building a connection and improving their likability. By being present in the moment, they can pick up on non-verbal cues, which allows them to better understand the message being relayed.

6. They show genuine interest.

Charismatic personalities know how to show genuine interest in others. They are not pretentious and have no issues working with those of a lower station than themselves. They are highly skilled at making the person they are talking to feel like they are the only other person in the world.

7. They are not narcissistic.

Instead of focusing on themselves, charismatic personalities know it's important to ask questions and dive deep into the minds of the people they are talking to. Not only do they make small talk, but they also ask deep, open-ended questions that can help uncover the emotions and motivations of others. This ties back to showing genuine interest in others.

8. They ask GOOD insightful questions.

Charismatic people understand the power of a good question. They tend to avoid asking closed or overly focused questions that lead only to short responses. Instead, they favor broad, open-ended inquiries that encourage detailed responses, opening up new avenues of conversation and deepening the connection. Take for example a charismatic leader at a business meeting. Instead of asking, "Did you meet your sales target?" which could result in a simple yes or no answer, they might ask, "Can you share your approach to reaching your sales target?" This kind of question provides room for a more comprehensive response and indicates a genuine interest in understanding the other person's experiences and strategies.

9. They offer genuine compliments.

Compliments are a powerful tool in the charismatic person's arsenal, particularly when they are sincere and focused on something the recipient has worked hard to achieve. A well-placed compliment can show recognition and appreciation, boosting the other person's self-esteem and creating a positive connection. For instance, a charismatic person might commend a colleague on the brilliant presentation they delivered, highlighting their excellent research skills and engaging delivery style.

10. They engage with emotions and feelings.

Last, but by no means least, charismatic people understand the importance of discussing emotions and feelings. They steer away from the mundane, and instead ask questions that tap into how people are feeling about their day, their life, and their aspirations. A simple shift from asking, "How was your day?" to "How did the experiences of your day make you feel?" can open up a whole new level of conversation. Simple yet powerful questions like this tap into the heart of a matter, which is essential for building relationships that are meaningful and lasting.

HOW TO UNLEASH YOUR CHARISMA

Many think charisma is inborn - a genetic trait. But evidence shows it can be learned and cultivated (much like empathy). Professor Antonakis found that much of our charisma stems from how we speak and what we say. (Antonakis, 2019) The premise is simple; if person A wants to increase their charisma, they need an observer, person B. To win B's attention, trust and reverence, A must communicate their ideas to B in ways they can understand, relate to and remember. Basically, A must form an emotional connection with B, and that's where these charisma-boosting tactics come in. Here are 12 charismatic tactics anyone can try.

VERBAL TACTICS

Use metaphors, similes and analogies.

Metaphors, similes, and analogies help us communicate a message in a simple and relatable manner. They evoke emotions and create vivid mental images, making the message more impactful. For example, this analogy from *Forrest Gump* is often used when we talk about the many choices we face in life: "Life is like a box of chocolates - you never know what you're gonna get." In other words, life offers many choices and surprises, much like a box of chocolates. Basically, we can enhance understanding and facilitate engagement by relating our message to experiences or concepts that our audience is familiar with.

Tell stories and anecdotes.

Stories and anecdotes are potent tools for captivating your audience and conveying your message effectively. I have used this tactic many times in this book; for example, in Chapter 5, where I told you about when I learned the importance of having effective communication skills. By sharing real-life stories and experiences from my life, it makes the message I am trying to convey more relatable, engaging, and memorable. People connect emotionally with stories, and this allows them to understand and internalize your ideas more deeply. That said, use this technique in moderation. Trying to relate to others by talking about your own experiences might come off as somewhat narcissistic, so don't go overboard.

You can find plenty of content, both in books and online, that explores how to become a great storyteller, but one simple tactic you can apply right away is to have a few "mini" stories rehearsed and ready to go. One short but captivating little story can be a game-changer if presented right, especially if it's something other people can relate to.

Employ contrast.

Contrast is an appropriate word to describe the differences we encounter in life. We are naturally attracted to the incongruity of things because it helps us understand them in greater detail. For example, apples and oranges are both fruits, but the differences in their color sets them apart. Using contract to define yourself and your ideas helps emphasize your identity and clarify your message. By highlighting the differences between your perspective and alternative viewpoints, you create a clear distinction and make your ideas stand out.

Ask rhetorical questions.

Rhetorical questions are used to elicit a reaction from others, not an answer. They help bring attention to a topic and force the listener(s) to think and reflect on it. For example, "What is the point of all this?" has no clear answer but forces us to think and is an effective way to put dramatic emphasis on something.

Rhetorical questions engage your audience cognitively, stimulating their thought processes and encouraging active participation. They also create anticipation and build suspense, leading to a more exciting and memorable experience.

Organize content into triads.

The rule of three is a powerful principle in communication. By grouping your content into triads, you make the message more concise, memorable, and impactful. People tend to remember things better when they are in triads; live, love, laugh; the three little pigs, etc. Scientists have found we can quickly recall things in our short-term memory if they are in three or four chunks. This is because it provides a clear structure that an audience can easily follow, allowing them to retain and recall key points more effectively. A simple way to employ this rule is by breaking down your message into three parts, listing three key takeaways or listing items or points in threes.

Demonstrate your moral convictions.

Show your intention to do the right thing by expressing your values, ethics, and principles. You inspire trust and admiration in others by consistently aligning your words and actions with moral convictions. This starts with knowing yourself, what your values are, and what you want out of life (see Chapter 3: Defining What You Want). If you don't know yourself, what you like/don't like, or what you want to get out of life, then how can you expect others to be on board with your goals? People like those who have a sense of direction and whose actions match up with what they say. In other words, charismatic people are authentic and sincere. They mean what they say and they say what they mean.

Reflect group sentiments.

Charismatic personalities listen actively to the concerns and opinions of others. Acknowledging and addressing these concerns demonstrates empathy and creates a sense of belonging. Emphasizing shared stories, desires, and struggles helps to foster a collective identity and strengthen the connection with the audience.

For example, if your team at work has some setbacks, you might tell them that you understand what they are going through because you are going through it too. You share the disappointment, demotivation, stress and tension they feel.

Set high expectations.

Charismatic people often set audacious goals for themselves, as well as their audience. By challenging others to strive for greatness, they encourage them to tap into their full potential. Setting high expectations communicates your belief in your audience's abilities and motivates them to surpass their own limitations.

Communicate confidence.

Confidence is the linchpin of charisma. It simply means having the ability to be comfortable in your own skin, despite your imperfections. Developing confidence involves taking a long, hard, realistic look at yourself and learning to like what you see. This gives you personal power and boosts your self-esteem so you can eliminate your negatives, accentuate your positives, and learn to love yourself more every day.

When it comes to setting high expectations, confidence allows you to communicate with assurance and conviction, inspiring others to follow in your vision and goals.

It reassures others that the high goals you set can indeed be achieved, which cultivates a belief in their own capabilities.

NON-VERBAL TACTICS

In addition to the above verbal tactics, Antonakis listed three non-verbal tactics that add richness to our communication and help boost charisma.

Gesture naturally.

Natural gestures, such as slight hand movements, can enhance your communication by adding emphasis, clarity, and punctuation to your verbal message. However, to truly make use of this, use gestures that are authentic to you and complement your message. For instance, use subtle hand, arm and body movements to convey your message and engage your listeners. Avoid using excessive or distracting gestures, as they may detract from your message.

Let your facial expressions do the talking.

Facial expressions are pivotal in conveying emotions and adding depth to your communication. Your face can express a range of emotions that can amplify the impact of your words. If you are passionate about something, your facial expressions as you talk about it will show just how passionate you are. That said, facial expressions are a double-edged sword. You need to be mindful of them and ensure they align with the tone and content of your message. Be genuine and expressive, as they make you more relatable and help your audience connect with you.

Animate your voice.

It probably goes without saying that the voice is a powerful communication tool. The way we use our voice greatly influences how our message is received. If you are enthusiastic about something, your voice will convey it. You might use volume to create emphasis, adjust pacing to build suspense, and strategically utilize pauses to let important points sink in. Learn how to modulate your voice to convey various emotions, highlight key points, and keep your listeners interested. Consider how to utilize all these aspects to effectively impart your message.

In addition to all these tactics, remember to:

1. Maintain eye contact to show confidence, sincerity, and engagement.
2. Use open body language, like standing tall, with uncrossed arms and a relaxed posture to convey approachability and openness.
3. Smile genuinely, as a sincere smile creates a positive and welcoming atmosphere, making you more relatable and likable to others. As most of us have experienced, a sincere smile is contagious.

4. Display enthusiasm and passion for your message through your facial expressions and body language. Your energy can be contagious and inspire others.
5. Maintain a confident stance, regardless of whether you're sitting or standing. It conveys authority and self-assuredness.
6. Subtly mirror and match your listener's body language and expressions to establish rapport and make them feel heard. Matching their energy level can help you connect faster and more deeply.
7. Adjust your physical proximity to create a sense of connection. Stand or sit at an appropriate distance to make others feel comfortable and engaged.
8. Listen actively and display empathy.

BONUS TACTICS: ADDITIONAL TECHNIQUES TO ENRICH YOUR CONVERSATIONS

Occasionally, the art of interaction calls for some special maneuvers - bonus tactics that can transform ordinary and mundane conversations into engrossing dialogues. Let's examine a few such techniques:

The Three A's Technique

One of the most effective ways to encourage and support the people around you is by practicing the three A's: **Appreciation, Applause,** and **Admiration**. When you express these sentiments sincerely and regularly, you're not only affirming the people but also building stronger bonds with them. A simple, "I appreciate you for your thoughtfulness," or, "I applaud you for your resilience," or, "I admire your ability to remain calm under pressure," can work wonders. Remember the key here is sincerity. If you don't mean it, don't say it.

Playful Worldbuilding Technique

Frankly, conversations don't always have to be bound by the parameters of reality! Sometimes, letting your imagination run wild can lead to the most engaging discussions. The Playful Worldbuilding Technique involves talking about your ideal life or situation, no matter how outlandish. It might be something like, "Imagine us, living in four different houses, in four different parts of the world, for the four different seasons - wouldn't that be wonderful?" This technique does not just spark intriguing conversations, but it also provides a playful and humorous element that can lighten the mood and strengthen connections.

Us Against the World Technique

Making sure you're on the same team as your conversation partner is a powerful way to foster unity and camaraderie. Instead of trying to outdo each other, adopt the 'Us Against the World' mindset. This involves framing conversations in terms of common goals and joint efforts. For instance, "Let's figure this out together," or, "We can achieve this goal if we work as a team." Not only does this technique encourage a sense of unity and cooperation, but it also promotes mutual respect and understanding.

The Secret Ingredient to Charisma and Conversation Skills - Self-Improvement

Believe it or not, the key to developing charisma and conversation skills is simple - work on improving yourself. Having a wealth of exciting experiences and stories to tell can prove invaluable when engaging in conversations, because it helps you relate better to those around you. So, take some time out every now and then to add more entertaining and interesting stories to your repertoire. Whether it's taking a cooking class or traveling to an exotic destination, any activity that adds value to your life will also help enhance your conversations.

These bonus tactics are the perfect addition to all the other techniques we've discussed so far. Don't forget - engaging conversation is not only about what you say but also how you say it. When communicating with others, make sure to use the right words and adopt the appropriate tone. This is how to ensure your interactions are warm and meaningful every time.

Finally, and I think we can all appreciate this - keep it simple. I know I've given you a lot of pointers on how to be more charismatic, but whatever tactics you choose to employ, keep it simple. The reason charismatic people are so alluring is because they know how to be irresistible. And a key factor that plays into this irresistibility is that they keep things simple. Whether it's what they say or do, they work to ensure it's straightforward and relatable enough for everyone to understand. Don't try to be mysterious. If you are clear, concise and compelling, your listeners will be entranced and feel connected with you, willing to accommodate your needs and share their own with you.

13

RULES OF INTIMACY TO LIVE BY

One might say that a relationship's ultimate goal is compassion. It can be difficult to find, but when it is found, even in small amounts, it can make a significant difference. Compassion includes attributes like empathy and benevolence, which not only impact how two people can develop in a relationship, but also can inspire them to develop toward one another.

This is why it's vital to learn about yourself and your motivations before becoming an effective communicator. A good analogy for this might be that it's impossible to begin construction on a home on the second story; first, the foundation and ground floor must be built.

The changes and suggestions offered in this chapter can substantially aid you in incorporating the laws of intimacy into your life.

RULE NUMBER 1: KEEP YOUR CIRCLE SMALL

One of my mentors once advised me, "Keep your circle small and be careful who you trust." This translates to fewer friends but less turmoil; it also implies being picky and specific, which is essential in today's world. If that means losing people who you've discovered were hiding their true identities behind a mask, it's unfortunate, but almost certainly for the best.

Personally, I have a small circle of friends who help me feel accepted and cherished. They admire my open heart, loyalty, compassion, problem-solving abilities, and so on. Most importantly, they approve of my decisions and express genuine delight in spending time with me.

Being a part of a larger group tends to include a lot of adjusting and impressing others. The fewer people you deal with, the less drama you have to deal with. Many friends may imply that they will be there in good times and bad, but only a handful will prove their sincerity.

Different views, cultures, and lifestyle habits are the general characteristics of a diverse group of people, but there are obvious drawbacks to this dynamic, such as competition for attention, teasing, misunderstandings, and so on. If you communicate your feelings to a large group of friends, you can't be sure that there isn't one among them who finds your troubles amusing or foolish. With a small group of friends, you usually get to know everyone so well that you can disclose secrets and fears without hesitation.

Research has shown that spending time with trustworthy friends increases happiness and improves mental health. To me, this is a good enough reason to 'keep my circle small.'

RULE NUMBER 2: GIVE 100 PERCENT COMMITMENT TO THOSE YOU LOVE

When you first start a relationship, you may find it difficult to commit right away. Even when you're in love, it takes time to create trust and strengthen the relationship. Commitment, on the other hand, is an essential component to keep the flame alive in a fulfilling and long-lasting relationship.

Each partner's sense of security depends on their commitment. Feeling safe encourages love, trust, and loyalty, and gives both people the courage to dream and plan for the future together.

Commitment does not imply the abolition of your independence or the loss of your identity. In fact, dedication in a relationship can help you become more robust during difficult circumstances. It's reassuring to know that you've got each other's backs when the going gets tough. In fact, dedication is as crucial as love and desire.

If you're not sure where to begin when it comes to staying committed in a relationship, writing a commitment statement can help. (Connors, 2019) In such a statement, the purpose and aims of the relationship are outlined. It may also include norms and boundaries that enhance the partnership and provide a sense of security to both parties.

RULE NUMBER 3: CUT OFF TOXIC RELATIONSHIPS

Although removing toxic people from your life isn't always easy, it's often the greatest thing you can do for your emotional and physical well-being. It may not take you long to figure out who or what in your life is unhealthy for you. Chances are, they manipulate or continuously criticize you. They may make you feel awful about yourself, even to the point where you engage in self-destructive behaviors as a result of their emotional or psychological abuse.

Despite all the warning signs, understanding and accepting how hazardous these relationships are can be difficult because you've convinced yourself that this person truly cares about your well-being. But it's imperative to figure out if a relationship is causing you considerable distress or has a negative impact on your mental health. Dispense with relationships that do not treat you the way you deserve to be treated.

Removing a toxic individual from your life is a challenging task that can cause a variety of uncomfortable emotions. It helps to have a good support system that you can rely on to help you get through this difficult period. Surround yourself with people who make you happy and encourage you. Reach out to friends and family members who will listen, affirm, and support you as you move forward without the toxic relationship weighing you down. (Connors, 2019) You might be surprised at how many of your true friends and caring family members will be there for you with open arms.

RULE NUMBER 4: SPEND ALONE TIME TOGETHER WITHOUT SOCIAL MEDIA

I don't think it's a surprise to anyone that most of us waste a lot of time on our phones and computers. But what's the big deal? You may be wondering why you should give up a habit that doesn't appear to be causing any problems.

The truth is that the negative consequences of all the time we spend on our phones might shock you. Here are a few alarming facts about cell phone usage:

- According to a University of Arizona study, teens engaged in high usage of a smartphone showed indicators of despair.
- According to a University of Pennsylvania study, as well as a number of other studies, reducing social media exposure can lead to considerable improvements in happiness.
- According to countless studies, smartphone use negatively affects our attention span and capacity to focus.

Not everyone is affected by cell phone use in the same way, of course, but spending too much time on our phone can harm our mental health, diminish our ability to focus, and cause relationship problems.

Both the iPhone and Android have capabilities that allow you to keep track of how much time you spend on your phone. You can check your daily average time spent, weekly total, and which apps you use most. Seeing how much time you spend on your phone each week might be a big eye-opener. This is particularly true when you consider all the other things you could have done with that time. Maybe you could have picked up a new hobby, started a side business to supplement your income, or simply spent more quality time with family or friends.

Creating a phone usage schedule for yourself is one approach to spending less time on your phone. Set aside certain times of the day when you won't be able to use your phone for anything other than essential communication. Then set certain hours when you can go through social media or play video games without feeling guilty.

Disable notifications. We may spend more time on our smartphones than we intend merely because of notifications. Consider the following scenario: you're working at your desk when you receive a notification that someone has posted on your most recent Instagram snap. You open the app to view the comment and respond in a matter of seconds. It happens all the time, but it isn't healthy to be constantly jumping to the dictates of your phone.

RULE NUMBER 5: FORGIVE WHEN YOU'RE OFFENDED

Anger and resentment can be neutralized by forgiveness. The Dalai Lama recommends that the best approach to deal with becoming upset after being wronged by someone is to look at them from a different perspective and determine if they have any redeeming characteristics. He also believes that unpleasant experiences might be a prime opportunity that would otherwise be unavailable, which is a type of positive reframing.

The Dalai Lama also tells us that "acceptance of suffering and injuries perpetrated by others" is a sort of patience and kindness that can be cultivated alongside an understanding of the complexity of the human situation and the nature of reality.

Another technique to deal with anger that aids in the cultivation of forgiveness is to focus on how we are all related, since we all share the feeling of pain and all want to be free of it.

The Buddhist perspective on wrath and resentment argues that practicing the virtue of forgiveness is intertwined with the development of patience and tolerance exercises. These types of practices include cultivating awareness and wisdom, as well as giving, compassion, and honesty.

RULE NUMBER *6*: IMPROVE YOURSELF DAILY - KEEP BEING VALUABLE AND WANTED

Being stuck in the same spot and feeling as if nothing is changing can be frustrating. It feels like you're not progressing toward your goals but are instead languishing. Taking action is one approach to getting out of such a rut. It can be inspiring and encouraging to make a conscious choice to better yourself. Working to better yourself can have a positive impact on your health, as well as your connections with family, friends, and colleagues.

Unfortunately, self-improvement occasionally gets a bad rap. Our ambition to improve ourselves has resulted in a burgeoning industry of poor hacks that can leave us feeling even more irritated than before. Alternatively, there are things that make us feel wonderful but don't propel us forward.

Make time to unwind. In other words, begin with the fundamentals before learning how to improve. Before you can move on to self-improvement, you must first meet your basic needs. Making time for rest is a big part of that. There are numerous types of relaxation. Find time in your calendar where you can just do nothing and chill out, even if only for a few minutes. Those calm minutes can assist you in decompressing and processing the day's events. Making time for relaxation will almost certainly be beneficial to your health. And when you're well-rested, you'll have more time to focus on other ways to improve yourself.

Consider reading more. Almost everything can be found in a book and reading more will help you unwind, entertain you, and maybe even illuminate new interests for you. A book can help you learn a new skill. Some books are written expressly to assist you on your journey of self-improvement and personal development. You can develop leadership skills by reading. Engrossing yourself in a fiction novel can transport you to other places or times, where you go with exciting characters. Basically, whatever interests you should be something you're reading about.

Begin a thankfulness routine. Being appreciative of what you have is one way to learn more about being a better person. Practicing thankfulness for what you have today can prevent you from feeling resentful about what you lack. You don't have to be appreciative of big things. Try to pay attention to the simple things that make you joyful and content. Over time, your appreciation practice will improve and expand. The more you do it, the easier it becomes to automatically think of things for which you're grateful.

Eat nutritious food. When you're healthy and well-fueled, it's easier to take the right steps toward what you desire in life. What we eat has a significant impact on our mood. Pay attention to what you put into your body. Eat a variety of foods in various colors across all food groups. When possible, try to eat fresh meals. If you don't have time to cook at home, consider other options, like meal kit memberships or healthy food service.

Increase the amount of movement in your life. Food might be an important influence on how you feel, but so is movement and exercise. There are numerous strategies available. You could begin a new sport and invite a friend to join you so you can spend time bonding. If this doesn't appeal to you, there are plenty of other ways to incorporate exercise into your life. Take a daily walk, go for a bike ride, join a dance class. You might even consider beginning a workout routine in the privacy of your own home. Many free fitness regimens are available online, so if you become bored with one, simply move on to another.

RULE NUMBER 7: EMBRACE VULNERABILITY IN YOUR RELATIONSHIPS

As we discussed earlier, vulnerability means taking a chance. You risk getting hurt for a chance at making a genuine connection. As we all know, opening up is not easy. If we share our insecurities, secrets, and fears, we are often afraid of how others will react. They might think differently about us or even reject us, which is something we don't want to risk.

However, with great risk comes great reward. Letting your guard down and letting yourself be vulnerable in your relationships by sharing your deepest fears, wildest dreams, or embarrassing stories increases intimacy, trust, and emotional connection. When you are vulnerable, you foster deeper understanding and empathy, which creates a sense of safety and comfort, which in turn increases relationship satisfaction and longevity.

Being vulnerable is difficult, of course, because it requires you to be open and honest, which can be uncomfortable and scary. Here are a few ways to open up more:

Recognize your emotions. Before you can be open and honest, you need to become aware of your own emotions, thoughts, and fears. As you work on being more forthcoming, take the time to contemplate your experiences to identify your feelings and the rationale behind them. This understanding will allow you to communicate more effectively.

Take things slowly. Vulnerability doesn't need to happen all at once. Begin with baby steps by opening up on smaller, less sensitive topics, then gradually move to topics that are more personal and intimate. This gradual approach is a great way to build your confidence and establish trust in the process.

Pick the right person. You should find someone you trust and feel safe with before opening up. Being vulnerable is hard and scary because you might be hurt or taken advantage of. That's why you need a safe and supportive person who makes you feel respected. This could be a close friend, family member, or your partner. Not everyone deserves your vulnerability, so only open up to those who have shown integrity and trustworthiness.

Practice active listening. Being vulnerable isn't only about sharing your life experiences but also listening and empathizing with others. Be an active listener and non-judgmental when somebody opens up to you, so you establish a safe space that encourages reciprocity and trust.

Challenge your fears. Don't let the fear of rejection, judgment, or criticism keep you from being vulnerable. Fear is natural, but it shouldn't dictate your actions.

Embrace imperfection. Understand that vulnerability is about being authentic and embracing your weaknesses.

Practice self-compassion. Being open with others requires self-compassion. You need to be easygoing and understanding toward yourself before you can open up to others. Recognize that feeling vulnerable is a natural part of human connection, so be patient and kind to yourself as you figure things out.

Rule number 8: Be Fully Present

In a world where so much is fighting for our attention, we crave having someone's full and undivided attention. That presence is so rare that when we finally have it, we feel seen, heard, and valued. Being more present is a valuable skill that can greatly enhance your well-being and your relationships.

Here's how to be more present in a world where so many of us are not paying enough attention:

Practice mindfulness. Mindful meditation is an excellent way to build up your present-moment awareness. Sit quietly and focus on the sensations of your breath, body, and surroundings. Use all your senses to anchor yourself in the present moment. As various thoughts arise, acknowledge them but bring your focus back to the present moment. Over time, this will allow you to be more fully engaged and present.

Slow down. In our fast-paced lives, we get caught up in rushing from one task to another. To be truly present, take intentional pauses throughout your day to slow down and be in the moment. For example, savor your meals by being mindful as you eat.

Limit your distractions. Minimize distractions that pull you away from the present moment. Stay away from your phone or turn off the notifications when you need to focus or spend quality time with others. Doing this will allow you to be an active listener, since it means you are consciously trying to be fully present.

Tackle one task at a time. Rather than multitasking, focus on one task at a time, give it your full attention, and immerse yourself in the experience.

Cultivate gratitude. Take time to reflect on and appreciate the present by focusing on what you are grateful for, whether big or small. Cultivating gratitude shifts your attention to the present and fosters a positive mindset.

14

WITTY BANTER TIPS AND TECHNIQUES

Interactions are filled with a variety of emotions. We all want to put our best foot forward and make a good first impression, and that's where light-hearted banter comes in. Research shows banter-related humor helps people feel more relaxed when they first meet and get to know each other. (Brooks et al., 2020)

Clever exchanges of humor and wordplay involve quick thinking and sharp wit. Engaging in light-hearted banter with another person adds an element of amusement, entertainment, and intellectual stimulation to conversations. People perceive those with good witty banter skills as naturally intelligent. It helps create a positive and enjoyable social atmosphere, fosters rapport, and can even be a tool for building relationships and connections.

In general, witty banter is characterized by the following:

- Clever wordplay – This involves the prevalent use of puns, clever phrasing, and double entendres to create humorous twists and turns in conversation.
- Quick thinking - Participants utilizing witty banter showcase their mental agility because they're able to respond promptly with clever comebacks and observations.
- Playfulness and humor - A light and playful tone is present, focusing on amusing and entertaining exchanges rather than serious discussion.
- Intellectual engagement - To appreciate and participate effectively in banter, you need a certain level of intelligence and cultural knowledge. Witty banter also challenges participants to think creatively and

analytically, encouraging the exploration of ideas, the use of wit, and the ability to make connections between seemingly unrelated concepts.

- Observational skills - Banter often involves keen observation of surroundings, people, and situations. Participants with sharp observational skills can make clever and relevant remarks that insert humor into any conversation.
- Versatility - Witty banter is adaptable to various contexts and topics, allowing participants to navigate a wide range of subjects, from light-hearted and trivial matters to more serious or intellectual discussions, while still maintaining a light-hearted tone.
- Nuance and subtlety - Banter is generally layered with subtle humor and hidden meanings. Its innuendos, wordplay, or cultural references require a degree of perceptiveness for one to fully appreciate it.
- Repartee - Witty banter involves a lot of back-and-forth exchanges, commonly known as repartee. This rapid and dynamic interplay of clever remarks and responses between participants creates an engaging and entertaining conversation.
- Positive intent - Banter is intended to evoke laughter, amusement, and enjoyment. It is never mean-spirited, disrespectful, or hurtful.

Benefits of Engaging in Witty Banter

Witty banter offers a variety of benefits, both on a personal and social level, including:

Social bonding. Banter is a powerful tool for creating and strengthening social connections. Sharing humor and witticisms can create a positive and enjoyable environment, fostering camaraderie and building rapport. (Kashdan et al., 2014) It can help break the ice, ease tension, especially when meeting someone for the first time, and establish a sense of familiarity and comfort in social interactions.

Enhanced communication skills. Mastering the art of witty banter enhances overall communication skills, since it applies skills like quick thinking, active listening, and the ability to respond promptly and cleverly. It also boosts your ability to articulate ideas, express yourself with precision, and adapt to different conversational styles.

Confidence and self-expression. Banter is a great way to show off your personality and boost your confidence in social settings. Delivering quick-witted remarks, making others laugh, and entertaining them cultivates self-assurance and a positive self-image. Expressing our thoughts and personality in this way helps us feel more at ease and assertive in social interactions.

Intellectual stimulation. Using wordplay, cultural references, and the exploration of clever ideas stimulates intellectual curiosity. It also encourages you to think critically, connect seemingly unrelated concepts, and showcase your knowledge and creativity. It keeps the mind active and sharp, fostering intellectual growth and expanding one's cultural repertoire.

Memorable interactions. Conversations filled with banter are more memorable and enjoyable. When you engage in clever and entertaining exchanges, it leaves a lasting impression. Being known for your wit also helps to create a positive reputation for you in your social and professional life.

Stress relief. Witty banter is a form of entertainment that can provide stress relief. It promotes laughter, boosts mood, and creates a positive emotional experience for everyone involved. By engaging in light-hearted and humorous exchanges with others, we can temporarily escape or alleviate stress.

Increased intimacy and closeness. Banter helps maintain closeness, intimacy, and comfort. Since you are able to talk more freely, openly, and honestly, even in serious situations, you connect on a deeper level. According to research, couples who banter are more likely to express satisfaction with each other. (Brauer & Proyer, 2018)

HOW TO USE WITTY BANTER IN CONVERSATION

As you can seen, bantering offers a plethora of perks, but using this technique varies depending on the situation and personalities involved. Whether it's with family, friends, intimate partners, or colleagues, banter lays the groundwork for longer, more meaningful interactions, allowing you to connect quicker and more deeply.

Here are some tips and techniques to help you master witty banter:

Understand different styles of banter.

There are different types of bantering styles. For example:

- Witty flirting - This is a form of playful and subtly suggestive conversation between people who have a romantic or sexual interest in each other. It involves witty exchanges, compliments, and playful teasing with a flirtatious undertone. For example:

Jackie: "I heard you're quite the chef. Any chance you can cook up a meal that's as tantalizing as your smile?"

Bill: "Oh, I don't know if I can live up to that, but I'm willing to give it a try. Just don't blame me if you fall head over heels for my cooking."

- Playful teasing - This is light-hearted teasing characterized by good-natured ribbing, often aimed at highlighting amusing quirks or little flaws of another. For example, if you are teasing your friend for having an old phone, you might say, "I can't believe you're still using that old phone. Are you waiting for it to become an antique?"

- Mild sarcasm - Sarcasm and irony are used to convey humor. For example:

Tom: "Wow, you're always right on time, Janice. I'm starting to think you might have a time machine."

Janice: "I do, and it doubles as a teleporter, so I can also instantly get away from boring conversations like this one."

- Self-deprecating humor - This involves making light-hearted jokes or remarks about yourself, often highlighting your own flaws or mistakes. To use this, you must be willing to laugh at yourself and not take yourself too seriously. Unlike aggressive humor that makes fun of others, self-deprecating humor creates a sense of humility, relatability, and approachability. If you are uneasy making witty remarks about something someone else has said, tell a little joke about yourself to ease the tension. For example:

Joey: "I can't believe I spilled coffee on myself again. I'm a walking disaster."

Peter: "Well, at least you're consistent. You should consider a career in modern art. Your coffee-stained shirts would fetch a fortune!"

Here, Joey playfully acknowledges his clumsiness by calling himself a "walking disaster." Peter then responds with his own remark that adds humor to the situation while lightening the mood.

- Goofy responses - These are whimsical, funny, and light-hearted responses meant to entertain or break the tension in a conversation. They are often spontaneous and can catch the other person off guard, eliciting laughter and creating a more joyful atmosphere. For example:

Julia: "What's your secret to staying young?"

Bryan: "Oh, it's simple. I bathe in a tub of rainbow sprinkles every morning and do the hokey pokey to keep my joints limber. Works like a charm!"

Know your audience.

On top of understanding the different types of banter, it's important to be aware that different types of banter work for different people and situations. For example, teasing someone you just met might not go over well, but teasing someone you are close with might be hilarious.

Diversify your knowledge of culture and topics.

The key to having engaging conversations is constantly learning new things. The more you expand your perspectives, the more you can relate to others. Try to stay updated on news and cultural trends that you're interested in, read books that stimulate conversation, or watch movies and talk shows, especially comedies. This will give you more material to work with.

Create unexpected connections between topics.

When trying to be clever, quick thinking is invaluable. If you can make connections between seemingly unrelated things, you have more creative and potentially humorous opportunities to take advantage of. For instance, a cup of coffee might remind you of a vacation or a nostalgic time. A dog or cat, depending on their characteristics, might remind you of a person.

Use your body.

Non-verbal gestures are powerful tools to use when bantering. Your body language and tone have to match your intention. They differ when making a witty remark, an awkward comment, or an accidental insult. For example, if you arrange to meet someone for lunch but when you see them you ask, "What are you doing here?" your body language and tone will determine how they take the question. If you're grinning and have a playful tone when you pretend to be surprised to see them despite inviting them to lunch, they'll understand you're kidding them.

Be positive and friendly.

Banter is not about being mean or rude. It's about being playful and respectful. Avoid sensitive or controversial topics unless you know the person well and they're comfortable with it. Also, remember to relax and have fun! Banter is supposed to be enjoyable, not stressful. If you feel nervous or pressured, try a relaxation hack like taking a deep breath, smiling, or listening to some music.

Be present and attentive.

Banter requires quick thinking and listening skills. You have to pay attention to what the other person is saying and respond accordingly. Don't become distracted by your phone or other stimuli around you.

Be confident and assertive.

Banter is a creative way of expressing yourself and your opinions. Don't be afraid to say what's on your mind, as long as it's appropriate and respectful. This can include standing up for yourself if someone tries to put you down or make fun of you in an unkind way.

Practice, practice, and practice some more.

The best way to improve your banter is to practice it with people you have a natural rapport with, like friends or family. You can also watch comedians, TV shows, or movies that feature witty dialogue and learn from them.

When banter becomes harmful.

Banter is not about hurting people's feelings or making them uncomfortable. It's about having fun and making others laugh. If something you said offended or upset someone, apologize sincerely and change the subject. Don't push their buttons or make fun of things they're sensitive about.

Often the most overlooked factor in cultivating successful relationships is the ability to make someone laugh. Who doesn't love having fun and laughing? Entertaining other people is a timeless skill, and that's why learning the art of witty banter is invaluable. If mastered, it can help you in all other areas of your life, including work, with friends, and in social settings.

TIME-TESTED TECHNIQUES TO ENHANCE YOUR CONVERSATIONAL BANTER

Now let's focus on introducing practical and actionable techniques for better conversation. These methods are not just theoretical but are tried and tested. The idea is to infuse a dash of wit and charm into your everyday dialogues, making them more interactive and engaging.

THE POWER OF OPEN-ENDED QUESTIONS

An open-ended question warrants a more detailed response from the other person, stimulating further conversation. For example, instead of asking someone if they enjoyed themselves at an event or function you both attended, in which the answer would likely be yes or no, ask them what specifically they enjoyed. This shows your interest in learning more about them and sparks a more in-depth conversation.

THE CHARM OF THE DOUBLE ENTENDRE

Remember Chandler Bing from *Friends*? As the quick-thinking, witty character, he often used double entendres - phrases or figures of speech that have two meanings or that could be understood in two ways. For example, maybe someone you know says, "Those people make good food." You might respond with something like, "I don't find people tasty at all." Or maybe you're with a friend who compliments you with, "You look really hot." You could retort, "Yeah, I'm sweating in this outfit!"

THE PLAYFUL MISUNDERSTANDING

Intentional misunderstanding can serve as a secret weapon in your conversational arsenal. For example, if someone sighs and says, "I've had a long day," you might respond, "Oh, was your day longer than 24 hours?" It's unexpected, and it lightens the mood, creating a more relaxed environment.

THE SURPRISE OF INTENTIONAL MISDIRECTION

Surprise is a useful element in engaging conversations. You can introduce this through intentional misdirection. Maybe a friend tells you they've landed a new job, but says it's hard to describe. You could say, "I get it, you could tell me but then you'd have to kill me, right?" This playful surprise response adds humor and livens up the conversation.

THE IMPACT OF VIVID AND IMAGINATIVE WORDS

Colorful and imaginative words can infuse humor and inventiveness into your dialogues. Instead of saying, "That's ridiculous," try "That's preposterous!" or replace "nonsense" with "poppycock." According to a study published in the *Journal of Personality and Social Psychology*, using more varied and imaginative language can make you more persuasive and can even increase your perceived credibility in the eyes of others.

THE TECHNIQUE OF BREAKING THE FOURTH WALL

This is a technique famously employed by characters in movies, like Ferris Bueller in *Ferris Bueller's Day Off*. In the middle of a conversation, he'll suddenly turn to the camera and comment directly to the viewer on whatever is happening in the moment. This adds a bit of silliness into any conversation and can lighten the mood when things become too serious.

THE SKILL OF GOING BEYOND THE LITERAL

Literal responses can often be boring. Why not spice things up? If someone asks what you do for a living, don't just tell them your job title. Try something like, "I juggle numbers and chase deadlines." It adds an element of the unexpected and makes your response more interesting.

Incorporating these techniques into our conversations fosters an atmosphere of playfulness and active engagement. The aim is to elevate every conversation, making each exchange enjoyable, memorable, and meaningful. After all, isn't that what all great conversations should be?

FINAL WORDS

"You miss 100% of the shots you don't take."
— WAYNE GRETZKY, ONE OF THE GREATEST ICE
HOCKEY PLAYERS EVER TO PLAY THE GAME

Gretzky's quote can be considered our guide through this entire journey, because it's applicable not just to hockey, or even sports, but to every aspect of life. Whether it's your personal life, work life, friendships, or romantic relationships, you have to take a chance. Without trying, without putting yourself out there, success eludes us.

I think this a perfect moment to pause and reflect. To look back at the path we've shared, the lessons we've learned, and how we can apply them to improve our everyday relationships.

Our journey was designed with one aim: to help you decode the winding, often puzzling world of interpersonal relationships and communication. My goal was to provide you with the right tools, effective strategies, and knowledge to aid you in your quest for more fulfilling and long-lasting relationships.

Let's take a moment now to review the four core aspects we explored in this book.

First, clarity is the foundation of our relationships. Imagine a crystal-clear lake. We can see everything beneath the water's surface, nothing is hidden or obscured. We need to seek this kind of clarity in our relationships – in our expectations of one another, the boundaries we set, and the way we communicate. Without it, we risk misunderstanding and conflict. This is where relationships often falter. The key is to have clear intentions and expectations so we can create a shared understanding and mutual respect that binds us together. If you don't know what you want, then you will never get it.

Our second section involved effective communication. As we know, communication works both ways: we need to speak to make our intentions known, but we also need to actively listen, showing empathy and understanding, and respond appropriately to what the other person is saying. The power of communication lies in its ability to create bonds between people, to bridge any differences and to find common ground. It helps us resolve conflicts, and is the medium through which we express our love and appreciation.

Overcoming obstacles was our third area of discussion. Dealing with difficult people, battling our own insecurities or fighting negative self-talk - these challenges aren't easy to overcome. But with the right mindset and the right tools, many of which you now have in your arsenal, we can move past these roadblocks to become stronger and more resilient.

Finally, we talked about how to be remarkable. Being remarkable doesn't mean being perfect. No one is perfect, and that's okay. Remarkability is about authenticity, and about making a positive, lasting impact on others. It's about continually striving to be the best version of ourselves, not just for our own happiness, but to enhance the quality of our relationships.

Each of these four principles build upon each other and form the bedrock of healthy, fulfilling relationships. I have provided you with instruments for developing healthier, more rewarding relationships, and now the responsibility is yours to use all you've learned here.

As Brené Brown once said, *"Courage starts with showing up and letting ourselves be seen."* Being courageous means allowing others to see us as we truly are. Embrace this courage. Make your presence felt in your relationships. Express your desires and needs with love and strength. Listen to others with empathy, and make an effort to see things from their perspective. Set your boundaries and maintain them, without feeling the need to apologize for having them. Above all, be unapologetically you. Be true to yourself.

As we've learned, cultivating relationships and mastering communication skills is not a sprint, but a marathon. It requires patience, persistence, and practice. You may stumble along the way, but every mistake or rejection is a lesson. The rewards - genuine, profound and long-lasting connections with others - are worth every bit of effort and every setback.

I urge you all to stand tall and seize every opportunity to nurture loving, lasting relationships. Use the insights you've gained from our journey here to be the best version of yourself, make new connections and strengthen old ones.

REFERENCES

5 Keys to Building Stronger Friendships In Adulthood. (n.d.). https://www.geneva.edu/blog/uncategorized/5-keys-to-building-better-friendships

Adler, Alfred. (1931, translated and reprinted 2010) What Life Should Mean To You. Martino Fine Books.

Amati, V., Meggiolaro, S., Rivellini, G., & Zaccarin, S. (2018). Social relations and life satisfaction: the role of friends. Genus, 74(1). https://doi.org/10.1186/s41118-018-0032-z

Andrew Bustamante. (2023, January 24). How to Become Irresistible | Andrew Bustamante [Video]. YouTube. https://www.youtube.com/watch?v=6cF-jrq-om0

Antonakis, J. (2019, February 7). Learning Charisma. Harvard Business Review. https://hbr.org/2012/06/learning-charisma-2

Banter And Wit: Everything You Need To Know. (2022). Get the Friends You Want. https://getthefriendsyouwant.com/banter-wit/

Big Think. (2023, March 31). The friendship recession | Richard Reeves [Video]. YouTube. https://www.youtube.com/watch?v=VpOan0hqdNA

Brandon, J. (2019, September 16). Science says there's a simple reason you keep thinking negative thoughts all day. Inc.com. Retrieved June 8, 2022, from https://www.inc.com/john-brandon/science-says-theres-a-simple-reason-you-keep-thinking-negative-thoughts-all-day.html

Brauer, K., & Proyer, R. T. (2018). To love and laugh: Testing actor-, partner-, and similarity effects of dispositions towards ridicule and being laughed at on relationship satisfaction. Journal of Research in Personality, 76, 165–176. https://doi.org/10.1016/j.jrp.2018.08.008

Brooks, A., Herrmann, P., & Andreas, S. (2020). The use of banter in psychotherapy: A systematic literature review. Counselling and Psychotherapy Research, 21(3), 570–586. https://doi.org/10.1002/capr.12361

Brower, T., PhD. (2022, January 16). How To Make Friends And Build Great Relationships At Work. Forbes. https://www.forbes.com/sites/tracybrower/2022/01/16/how-to-make-friends-and-build-great-relationships-at-work/?sh=2eb0d3ad7c8b

Buckley, D. (2022, April 6). Four common temperament styles. BetterHelp. Retrieved June 8, 2022, from https://www.betterhelp.com/advice/temperament/4-most-common-temperament-types/

Cherry, K. (2021, December 1). 6 different types of relationships you may find yourself in. Verywell Mind. Retrieved June 8, 2022, from https://www.verywellmind.com/6-types-of-relationships-and-their-effect-on-your-life-5209431

Chesak, J. (2018, December 10). The No BS Guide to setting healthy boundaries in real life. Healthline. Retrieved June 8, 2022, from https://www.healthline.com/health/mental-health/set-boundaries

Chris Williamson. (2022a, January 10). How To Build Genuine Charisma And Confidence - Charlie Houpert | Modern Wisdom Podcast 420 [Video]. YouTube. https://www.youtube.com/watch?v=XieCU9nzrl8

Chris Williamson. (2022b, January 14). How To Confidently Flirt With Women - 3 Principles [Video]. YouTube. https://www.youtube.com/watch?v=vO7Ylk5it2A

Christakis, N. and Fowler, J; (2009) The Surprising Power of our Social Networks and how They Shape Lives. Little, Brown.

Clark, B. (2019, August 23). What Makes People Charismatic, and How You Can Be, Too. The New York Times. https://www.nytimes.com/2019/08/15/smarter-living/what-makes-people-charismatic-and-how-you-can-be-too.html

Connors, C. D. (2019, February 10). The 5 keys to commitment in relationships. Medium. Retrieved June 8, 2022, from https://medium.com/the-mission/the-5-keys-to-commitment-in-relationships-bf20b67abdb4

Council, F. A. (2020, February 13). Council post: 12 methods to identify and fix communication problems within a team. Forbes. Retrieved June 8, 2022, from https://www.forbes.com/sites/forbesagencycouncil/2020/02/13/12-methods-to-identify-and-fix-communication-problems-within-a-team/?sh=11b42c977dbc

Curtis, N. (2022). Witty Banter: What it is & 15 Secrets to Talk Witty & Make People laugh. LovePanky - Your Guide to Better Love and Relationships. https://www.lovepanky.com/my-life/work-and-office/witty-banter-master

DeWitt, H. (2023). How to create and maintain strong friendships: The importance of strong bonds and tips on staying close. Thriveworks. https://thriveworks.com/help-with/relationships/keep-and-maintain-strong-friendships/

FINN agency. (2021, December 12). 12 proven tactics to become more charismatic - FINN agency - Medium. Medium. https://medium.com/@finn.brussel/12-proven-tactics-to-become-more-charismatic-6574f7a316c9

Fiske, S. T. (2016). How warmth and competence inform your social life. In Cambridge University Press eBooks (pp. 369–372). https://doi.org/10.1017/cbo9781316422250.080

Freeman, J., Stolier, R. M., Ingbretsen, Z. A., & Hehman, E. (2014). Amygdala Responsivity to High-Level Social Information from Unseen Faces. The Journal of Neuroscience, 34(32), 10573–10581. https://doi.org/10.1523/jneurosci.5063-13.2014

Goodtherapy.org. 0 Communication Problems and Mistakes We All Make - GoodTherapy.org Therapy Blog. (n.d.). Retrieved June 8, 2022, from https://www.goodtherapy.org/blog/10-communication-problems-and-mistakes-we-all-make-0919157/amp/

Gurteen, David. View all posts by David Gurteen, by, P., Gurteen, D., View all posts by David Gurteen, Says:, R., & says:, D. G. (2022, April 9). We humans are complex. Conversational Leadership. Retrieved June 8, 2022, from https://conversational-leadership.net/we-human-beings-are-complex/

Hailey, L. (2023). Be an Expert at Witty Banter…How to Charm With Your Words. Science of People. https://www.scienceofpeople.com/witty-banter/

Haller, M., & Hadler, M. (2006). How Social Relations and Structures can Produce Happiness and Unhappiness: An International Comparative Analysis.

Social Indicators Research, 75(2), 169–216. https://doi.org/10.1007/s11205-004-6297-y

Harbinger, Jordan. (April 25, 2022) 8 signs it's time to cut a toxic person out of your life (and how to do it). Retrieved June 8, 2022, from https://www.jordanharbinger.com/8-signs-its-time-to-cut-a-toxic-person-out-of-your-life-and-how-to-do-it/

Harvard Second Generation Grant and Glueck Study. (n.d.). Harvardstudy. https://www.adultdevelopmentstudy.org/grantandglueckstudy

Helpguide. (2022, May 6). Improving family relationships with emotional intelligence. HelpGuide.org. Retrieved June 8, 2022, from https://www.helpguide.org/articles/mental-health/improving-family-relationships-with-emotional-intelligence.htm

Heritage Healthcare. (2019, July 3). The importance of companionship. Retrieved June 8, 2022, from https://heritagehealthcare.co.uk/importance-of-companionship/#:~:text=Having percent20a percent20companion percent20in percent20life,as percent20well percent20as percent20reminisce percent20memories.

Heston, Klare; L. C. S. W. (2020, November 9). How to get to know yourself. wikiHow. Retrieved June 8, 2022, from https://www.wikihow.com/Get-to-Know-Yourself?amp=1

Holmes, L. (2017, December 7). 11 signs of a genuine friendship. HuffPost. Retrieved June 8, 2022, from https://www.huffpost.com/entry/qualities-of-real-friends_n_5709821/amp

Hoshaw, C. (2022, May 2). Join Healthline and Psych Central's 10-day Digital Disconnect Challenge. Healthline. Retrieved June 8, 2022, from https://www.healthline.com/health/mental-health/the-benefits-of-a-social-media-break-plus-30-things-to-do-instead

Jacob, C. (2020, October 6). How to love and accept yourself as you are. UpJourney. Retrieved June 8, 2022, from https://upjourney.com/how-to-love-and-accept-yourself

Kalish, A. (2022, March 18). 20 ways to improve yourself (and your life) in 30 minutes or less. The Muse. Retrieved June 8, 2022, from https://www.themuse.com/amp/advice/16-small-ways-you-can-improve-your-life-in-less-than-30-minutes

Kashdan, T. B., Yarbro, J., McKnight, P. E., & Nezlek, J. B. (2014). Laughter with someone else leads to future social rewards: Temporal change using experience sampling methodology. Personality and Individual Differences, 58, 15–19. https://doi.org/10.1016/j.paid.2013.09.025

King, P. (2020). The Art of Witty Banter. Pkcs Media, Incorporated.

Kishore, K. (2021). How To Communicate Better With The Rule Of Three. Harappa. https://harappa.education/harappa-diaries/the-rule-of-three/

Kristenson, S. (2022). 13 Steps to Get Along with Difficult People. Happier Human. https://www.happierhuman.com/difficult-people/

Kos, B. (n.d.). You need to love yourself first before you can truly love others. AgileLeanLife. Retrieved June 8, 2022, from https://agileleanlife.com/you-need-to-love-yourself-first-before-you-can-truly-love-others/amp/

Lewandowski , G. (2023, June 13). 3 Simple Ways to Improve Any Relationship | Psychology Today. Www.psychologytoday.com. https://www.psychologytoday.com/us/blog/the-psychology-of-relationships/202306/3-easy-ways-to-improve-any-relationship

Lewis Howes. (2022, February 25). PSYCHOLOGICAL TRICKS To Be More Charismatic & Confident TODAY! | Vanessa Van Edwards [Video]. YouTube. https://www.youtube.com/watch?v=iApkwoskJkc

Long, C., and Averill, J. (March 5, 2003) Solitude: An Exploration of Benefits of Being Alone. Wiley Online Library. https://onlinelibrary.wiley.com/doi/abs/10.1111/1468-5914.00204.

Markway, B. (2015, March 3). 20 Expert Tactics for Dealing With Difficult People | Psychology Today. www.psychologytoday.com. https://www.psychologytoday.com/us/blog/living-the-questions/201503/20-expert-tactics-for-dealing-with-difficult-people

McCoy, K. (2022, November 8). 7 Tips for Building Friendships to Last a Lifetime | Psychology Today. Www.psychologytoday.com. https://www.psychologytoday.com/us/blog/complicated-love/202211/7-tips-building-friendships-last-lifetime

Mindbodygreen. (2021, June 28). 11 Qualities Of A Good Friend & The Types Of "Friends" To Avoid. Mindbodygreen. https://www.mindbodygreen.com/articles/how-to-be-a-good-friend

Mind Tools Content Team By the Mind Tools Content Team, Team, the M.

T. C., wrote, Y., wrote, M., & wrote, M. (n.d.). Building good work relationships: Making work enjoyable and productive. From MindTools.com. Retrieved June 8, 2022, from https://www.mindtools.com/pages/article/good-relationships.htm

Mora-Ripoll, R. (2010, December 1). The therapeutic value of laughter in medicine. PubMed. https://pubmed.ncbi.nlm.nih.gov/21280463/

Morin, D. A. (2021, July 23). How To Banter (With Examples For Any Situation). SocialSelf. https://socialself.com/blog/how-to-banter/

Morningstar, A. (2022, April 22). 12 boundaries you ought to set in your relationship. A Conscious Rethink. Retrieved June 8, 2022, from https://www.aconsciousrethink.com/6573/boundaries-in-relationships/

Myers, D. G. (2000). The funds, friends, and faith of happy people. American Psychologist, 55(1), 56–67. https://doi.org/10.1037/0003-066x.55.1.56

Natalie. (2021, December 7). What is healthy and unhealthy boundaries? faq. Retrieved June 8, 2022, from https://faq-ans.com/en/Q percent26A/page=a059eb640687f9701066551ff9c6cb7d

Nordquist, R. (2019, September 19). Learn the art of communication and see how it's used effectively. ThoughtCo. Retrieved June 8, 2022, from https://www.thoughtco.com/what-is-communication-1689877

Norris, Rebecca. Headshot 1 Jan 14, 2021 @ 4:18 pm. (n.d.). 9 ways to set boundaries with your family without getting into a full-blown argument. HelloGiggles. Retrieved June 8, 2022, from https://hellogiggles.com/love-sex/family/how-to-set-boundaries-with-family/

O'Donovan, Kirstin; Certified Life and Productivity Coach. (March 2, 2021) 10 negative thoughts we all have and what to think instead. Lifehack. Retrieved June 8, 2022, from https://www.lifehack.org/articles/communication/10-negative-thoughts-all-have-and-what-should-think-instead.html

Parienti, S. (2020, June 13). Setting a clear intention percent. YOGI TIMES. Retrieved June 8, 2022, from https://www.yogitimes.com/article/setting-clear-intention-alignment-love-relationships

Pogosyan, M. (2019, February 22). Is Charisma a Gift—or Can It Be Trained? | Psychology Today. Www.psychologytoday.com. https://www.psychologytoday.com/us/blog/between-cultures/201902/is-charisma-gift-or-can-it-be-trained

Psychology Today. (n.d.). Charisma | Psychology Today. Www.psychologytoday.com. Retrieved July 12, 2023, from https://www.psychologytoday.com/us/basics/charisma

Rethink.org. (n.d.) Negative thinking: What is negative thinking and how can I get help? Retrieved June 8, 2022, from https://www.rethink.org/advice-and-information/about-mental-illness/learn-more-about-symptoms/negative-thinking/

Salters-Pedneault, Kristalyn. P. D. (n.d.). You can regain emotional stability in BPD. Verywell Mind. Retrieved June 8, 2022, from https://www.verywellmind.com/reduce-your-emotional-instability-425375

Sample, I. (2018, February 14). Human brain subliminally judges "trustworthiness" of faces. The Guardian. https://www.theguardian.com/science/2014/aug/06/brain-subliminally-judges-trustworthiness-faces

Sasson, R. (2021, December 9). 12 relationship goals to make your love deeper and stronger. Success Consciousness | Positive Thinking - Personal Development. Retrieved June 8, 2022, from https://www.successconsciousness.com/blog/relationships/relationship-goals/

Social Connection — Current Priorities of the U.S. Surgeon General. (n.d.). https://www.hhs.gov/surgeongeneral/priorities/connection/index.html

Society19. (2019, February 25). 8 reasons to Keep Your Circle Small. Retrieved June 8, 2022, from https://www.society19.com/reasons-to-keep-your-circle-small/amp/

Tehran Times. (2017, August 16). Phlegmatic temperament: Specifications and lifestyle. Tehran Times. Retrieved June 8, 2022, from https://www.tehrantimes.com/news/415977/Phlegmatic-temperament-Specifications-and-lifestyle

The State of American Friendship: Change, Challenges, and Loss - The Survey Center on American Life. (2022, April 7). The Survey Center on American Life. https://www.americansurveycenter.org/research/the-state-of-american-friendship-change-challenges-and-loss/

Tom Bilyeu. (2023, January 19). How To SEDUCE & INFLUENCE Anyone

With Psychology - TRY THIS & SEE RESULTS | Vanessa Van Edwards [Video]. YouTube. https://www.youtube.com/watch?v=lrrYFQN_CTI

Tousley, S. (2022, August 31). How to Be Charismatic: The 9 Habits of Insanely Likable People. Hubspot.com. https://blog.hubspot.com/sales/habits-of-likable-people

Van Edwards, V. (2022). The Charismatic Personality: 12 traits you can master. Science of People. https://www.scienceofpeople.com/charismatic-traits/

Warren, R. (2018). 10 Ways To Build Stronger Friendships in Your 20s. GenTwenty. https://gentwenty.com/ways-to-build-stronger-friendships-in-your-20s/

Wertheim, Edward G; (n.d.) The Importance of Effective Communication. Northeastern University, College of Business Administration. chrome-extension://efaidnbmnnnibpcajpcglclefindmkaj/https://ysrinfo.files.wordpress.com/2012/06/effectivecommunication5.pdf

WhatMaster. (2020, December 13). What are human relationships? types, importance, objectives,..ETC. Retrieved June 8, 2022, from https://whatmaster.com/human-relationships/amp/

Winston, J. S., Strange, B. A., O'Doherty, J. V., & Dolan, R. J. (2002). Automatic and intentional brain responses during evaluation of trustworthiness of faces. Nature Neuroscience, 5(3), 277–283. https://doi.org/10.1038/nn816

Yang, Y., Boen, C., Gerken, K., Li, T., Schorpp, K. M., & Harris, K. M. (2016). Social relationships and physiological determinants of longevity across the human life span. Proceedings of the National Academy of Sciences, 113(3), 578–583. https://doi.org/10.1073/pnas.1511085112